THE HOLIDAY DESSERT BOOK

Also by Kathy Cutler

The Festive Bread Book

THE HOLIDAY DESSERT BOOK

NEARLY 200
DELECTABLE TREATS
FOR A YEAR
OF CELEBRATIONS

KATHY CUTLER

PHOTOGRAPHS BY JOHN UHER

MACMILLAN PUBLISHING COMPANY • NEW YORK

Library of Congress Cataloging-in-Publication Data
Cutler, Kathy.
The holiday dessert book.
Includes index.
1. Desserts. 2. Holiday cookery. I. Uher, John.
II. Title.
TX773.C85 1986   641.8'6   86-12833
ISBN 0-02-529300-1

Macmillan Publishing Company
866 Third Avenue, New York, N.Y. 10022
Collier Macmillan Canada, Inc.

Macmillan books are available at special discounts
for bulk purchases for sales promotions, premiums,
fund-raising, or educational use. For details, contact:
Special Sales Director, Macmillan Publishing
Company, 866 Third Avenue, New York, New York
10022

10 9 8 7 6 5 4 3 2 1

Printed in the United States of America

DESIGNED BY BARBARA MARKS

To my husband, Charles,
and my children,
Chase and Pam

CONTENTS

ACKNOWLEDGMENTS

My thanks for the assistance I needed to complete this book go to the following:

The Arthur and Elizabeth Schlesinger Library on the History of Women in America, Cambridge, Massachusetts. The kindness of its staff and the convenience of its wide-ranging research materials could hardly be surpassed.

The staff of Levi E. Coe Library, Middlefield, Connecticut, under the direction of Dorothy Smith, for obtaining many of the books I required in my research, with special gratitude to Martha McCormick.

Jane Wilson of JCA Literary Agency, my agent, who offered valued advice and encouragement.

Andrea Raab, formerly of Macmillan, who supplied the enthusiasm that helped launch this book.

Emily Easton, my editor, who has been consistently thorough and helpful.

Charlotte R. Gross for an excellent job of copyediting the manuscript.

Betty Gross of Middletown, Connecticut, who has helped me with many recipes.

And especially Charles L. Cutler, my husband, who worked with me on every phase of the book—planning, research, writing, editing, and typing. His efforts made this book possible.

INTRODUCTION

While writing a book on the breads traditionally associated with holidays, I became aware that a significant number of desserts are similarly linked with holidays. My research over the past several years has yielded a wealth of holiday dessert recipes from various religions, countries, cultures, and even eras.

Holiday desserts include cakes, cookies, pies, tarts, puddings, and candies. They incorporate an astonishing array of fruits, nuts, sweets, spices, and liqueurs. Some are simple to prepare, others are elaborate. But they are all excellent: people reserve the best for their holiday celebrations.

Many of the original recipes from which I've worked are old-fashioned in their vagueness about measurements, or require ingredients not readily available, or are sometimes apparently not workable. All the recipes in this book have been tested, revised, and adapted for the contemporary cook. Yet, refined though they often are, the recipes are true to the originals.

Among the pleasures of these desserts, I've found, is that they enhance the charm of festive occasions. Easter paskha, Thanksgiving Indian pudding, and Christmas mince pie all add to the joy of the holidays they accompany. At a time when many traditions seem threatened by rapid social change, such time-honored delicacies are welcome reminders of a past we wish to remember. I've given the historical background of the desserts throughout, explaining their traditional presentations.

THE
HOLIDAY
DESSERT
BOOK

1

TIPS ON MAKING DESSERTS

Desserts are the crowning touch of a fine meal. They add to, not dominate, the dishes that precede them. The ideal dessert may be sweet but not cloying; rich but not heavy; flavorful but not too strong; complex but not fussy. Follow these suggestions for desserts that will leave the diners at your table looking forward to a return engagement.

Simple Ingredients

Flour

- I recommend *all-purpose flour,* unbleached, for nearly all the recipes that contain flour. All-purpose flour is a wheat flour coarser than cake flour. But the mixture of hard and soft wheat in all-purpose flour makes for a texture that enhances the flavor of a dessert.
- *Cake flour* consists of soft wheat that is lower in gluten. It yields a more tender, finer texture.
- *Self-rising flour* contains baking powder and salt, which make a cake more tender.
- *Rye flour,* usually combined with wheat flour, comes in grades of white, medium, and dark.

Leavening

- The *baking powder* used is the standard double-acting kind. Batter containing it rises when a liquid is added and again when the batter is heated—making for an evenly leavened dessert. *Make sure baking powder is fresh!* Replace can about 6 months after opening.

• *Baking soda* is a leavener used in recipes containing an acid ingredient such as sour milk, molasses, or honey.

Butter
The recipes call for regular butter, which is lightly salted. You may use margarine or unsalted butter if you wish. The role of butter, shortening, and other fats is to provide flavor, tenderness, and texture.

Milk and Cream
Use regular, whole milk in your desserts. Cream means heavy cream, unless otherwise noted.

Eggs
Use large eggs in all the recipes. It doesn't matter whether the eggs are brown or white. Eggs add flavor, color, and texture to desserts.

Sugar and Sweetening
• Use granulated, confectioners', brown, or cube *sugar* as recommended. Sugar adds taste, flavor, and texture to desserts.

• *Molasses* and *honey* are the only other sweeteners used here. Each contributes a distinctive flavor to a dessert.

Chocolate and Cocoa
• Normally use semisweet or unsweetened chocolate as indicated. Adds flavor, taste, and color to dessert.

• Use only the unsweetened cocoa powder made for cooking. Adds flavor, taste, and color.

Nuts
Nuts provide distinctive taste or texture. Sample to make sure they're fresh! (Leftover nuts freeze well.)

Rosewater
Used especially in Middle Eastern recipes for a unique haunting flavor. Obtainable in many gourmet shops, pharmacies, and suppliers of Middle Eastern foods.

Phyllo Dough
Is a thin and flaky pastry used for baklavá and a variety of other desserts. It can be bought in most grocery stores.

Prepared Ingredients
Pie Crust

> 2 cups all-purpose flour
> ½ teaspoon salt
> 6 tablespoons shortening
> 4–5 tablespoons ice water
>
> 9-inch pie plate

1. In a mixing bowl, combine flour and salt. Cut in shortening with two knives or a pastry blender until mixture looks like coarse meal.

2. Gradually add cold water 1 tablespoon at a time, tossing with a fork after each addition. Continue until dough can be gathered into a ball. Wrap ball in foil or plastic wrap. Refrigerate at least 30 minutes. Roll out and put in a pie plate.

NOTE: Cover edges with aluminum foil to prevent overbrowning.

Almond Paste
You can buy almond paste in gourmet sections of supermarkets. Or you can make your own as follows:

> 3 cups slivered almonds
> 3 cups confectioners' sugar
> ½ cup water
> 1 teaspoon almond extract
>
> blender or food processor

If you use a blender to grind almonds, put ½ cup of almonds at a time in container. Grind almonds until very fine. In a large bowl, combine ground almonds with remaining ingredients. Use fingers to mix. Knead until smooth. Use, or keep in refrigerator or freezer.

If you use a food processor to grind almonds, insert steel

blade. Add almonds and process until finely ground. Add remaining ingredients. Process until mixture forms a ball. Use, or keep in refrigerator or freezer.

Vanilla Sugar

Place a vanilla bean broken in small places into 1 cup of sugar. Store in a tightly covered jar about 10 days. Sift before using.

Utensils

Bundt pan: Originally designed for a classic German cake, this round, fluted pan is used for making a variety of unfrosted cakes. There are two sizes for cakes: 8 by 3 inches (6 cups) and 10 by 4 inches (12 cups). Good for angel food cake, coffee cake, and breads.

Springform pan: Mold or pan with a rim fastened to the bottom with a spring or clamp. This can be released to remove the rim, allowing food to be taken out easily. Available in various sizes.

Cake pan: Round, square, or rectangular. It's useful to have several.

Loaf pan: Those used here are 9 by 5 inches. If you use a smaller size, shorten cooking time. Useful for many cakes as well as for bread.

Flan pan: This pan, with a raised bottom, makes a cake with a rim that can hold fruit or a filling.

Tart mold (tiny): Fluted form for making bite-size Swedish sandtarts or Pennsylvania Dutch Christmas cookies.

Pie plate: Nine-inch aluminum or glass pie plates are used for the pie recipes. The 8- or 10-inch sizes are all right, too. If you use a glass pie plate, lower oven temperature by 25°F.

Baking sheet: Used in this book mainly for cookies.

Jelly-roll pan: Has sides about 1 inch high. Used for a Yule log and other desserts.

Cookie cutter: Choose from hundreds of different shapes and sizes. I prefer plastic over metal cutters because of greater detail.

Springerle rolling pin or springerle board: Imprints designs on Christmas cookies.

Speculaas cookie plank: Traditional wooden mold for making this classic Dutch cookie. Comes in quaint designs and is often displayed as a kitchen ornament.

Rolling pin: My preference is for a narrow, solid wooden rolling pin about 19 inches long, and with tapering ends, for good control. But many people opt for the heavy ball-bearing wooden pin with handles. There are mixed reports on the effectiveness of marble rolling pins.

Wire rack: For cooling cakes and cookies.

Pantry brush or feather: For applying glaze or melted butter or for brushing away excess flour. Many prefer the feather because it is easier to work into corners and to clean.

Pastry blender: Device with handle and curved metal blades for cutting shortening into flour. Or use two table knives.

Pastry bag: Plastic-lined, sometimes nylon bag in different sizes for frosting cakes or applying whipped cream to desserts. Many prefer the larger size because it holds more filling.

Rosette-timbale iron: Iron mold, with detachable handle, for frying cookies of various shapes.

Techniques

Bake: Cook in oven, which should be preheated about 10 minutes before baking.

Deep frying: Should be done in a special deep-frying pan with a wire basket and lid. A slotted spoon is handy for removing food. To prevent boiling over, don't fill pan more than halfway and don't fry more than 3 or 4 pieces of dough at a time. Watch during cooking to prevent overflow and possible fire. Have metal lid and salt handy to smother flames should fat catch fire. (Don't use water, which would spread the flames.)

If you don't have a deep fryer, put about 2 inches of vegetable oil in a deep saucepan and heat to about 375°F before using.

Steaming: In this technique, steam from boiling water serves to cook desserts such as plum pudding.

Beat: Mix air into batter. An electric mixer is most common, but you may use a rotary beater or wire whisk. A wooden spoon is sometimes used with thicker batter.

Whip: Beat briskly to lighten mixture and increase volume.

Blend: Mix ingredients well.

Stir: Mix with circular motion, usually using a spoon.

Fold: Mix by gently turning one ingredient over the other, often with a rubber spatula.

Cream: Beat until light and fluffy.

Knead: Work dough with hands to make smoother.

Roll out: Shape and thin dough with a rolling pin.

Glaze: Brush top of dessert with milk, cream, egg, egg white, or jelly to give sheen.

Further Tips

General

1. Read recipe carefully and thoroughly before starting to cook.

2. Never substitute oil for butter or margarine, unless recipe so states.

3. Brown sugar should always be firmly packed when measured.

4. Unless otherwise noted, all ingredients should be at room temperature.

5. To save time, chop nuts and fruits to desired size and keep in labeled jars.

6. Do you wonder whether your baking power is fresh? Add 1 teaspoon of the baking powder to ⅓ cup of warm water. If the water fizzes, the baking powder is all right. Otherwise, it's not active and should be replaced.

7. If shredded coconut is dried out, freshen it in a vegetable steamer over boiling water.

8. To plump raisins, soak them 5 to 10 minutes in the liquid used in the recipe. Drain and reserve for later use in recipe. Pat raisins dry before using.

9. To toast shredded coconut or almonds, bake in a preheated 350°F oven 10 to 15 minutes.

Cookies

1. To keep drop cookies from spreading together, chill dough and drop 2 inches apart.

2. To prevent bar cookies from becoming hard and crusty, use correct size of pan and do not overbake.

3. To prevent bar cookies from becoming doughy, do not use a pan that is too small; check for doneness before removing from oven.

4. To keep soft cookies from becoming hard, store in an airtight container. If cookies become dried out, put an apple half into container to restore moisture.

5. To prevent crisp cookies from becoming soft, keep in loosely covered container in a cool dry place.

6. The flavor of dry cookies containing dried fruit and spices often improves after several weeks of storage.

7. Baked cookies in small packages freeze well for up to 3 to 4 months.

8. To shape small cookies, or to make 1-inch ball cookies, use a tiny ice cream scoop.

Cakes

1. To ensure distribution of chopped nuts, dried fruits, or dates throughout a cake, mix them with a small amount of flour before adding to batter.

2. Age fruitcakes before serving to ensure mellow flavor and smooth slicing.

3. To prevent a cake from sticking to the pan, grease and flour pan sufficiently, covering entire inner surface.

4. For best results, freeze cakes without frosting. A cake with buttercream frosting may be frozen if toothpicks are inserted on the top and sides of the cake to prevent wrapping from sticking.

5. To prevent overflowing, never fill cake molds more than halfway.

6. To make cake layers of even size (same height), use a measuring cup to fill pans alternately, ½ cupful at a time.

7. To prevent a cake from crumbling, cool in pan 10 minutes after baking. Then cool on a wire rack.

Pies

1. To keep a pie shell from puffing up while baking, prick the pastry. Then line with foil and fill with dried beans. Shortly before completion of baking, remove foil and beans.

2. In making pie crust, add less than the required amount of water. Then add a drop or two at a time as needed.

3. Don't handle dough too much—this increases gluten content and toughness.

For the flaming of desserts, see page 253.

Table of Weights and Measures

A pinch equals the amount that can be picked up and held between thumb and forefinger, about ⅛ teaspoon.

60 drops	= 1 teaspoon	2 cups	= 1 pint (16 ounces)
3 teaspoons	= 1 tablespoon	4 cups	= 32 ounces
2 tablespoons	= 1 ounce or ⅛ cup		= 1 quart
4 tablespoons	= ¼ cup	4 quarts	= 1 gallon
8 tablespoons	= ½ cup	8 quarts (dry)	= 1 peck
16 tablespoons	= 1 cup	4 pecks (dry)	= 1 bushel
	= ½ pint		
	= 8 ounces		

Conversion Tables for Metric Measurements

Liquid Measures
(1 liter = 10 deciliters (dl) = 100 centiliters (cl)
= 1,000 milliliters (ml)

Spoons, cups, pints, and quarts	Liquid ounces	Metric equivalent
1 tsp	$\frac{1}{16}$ oz	$\frac{1}{2}$ cl; 5 ml
1 Tb	$\frac{1}{2}$ oz	15 ml
$\frac{1}{4}$ c; 4 Tb	2 oz	$\frac{1}{2}$ dl; 59 ml
$\frac{1}{3}$ c; 5 Tb	$2\frac{2}{3}$ oz	$\frac{3}{4}$ dl; 79 ml
$\frac{1}{2}$ c	4 oz	1 dl; 119 ml
1 c	8 oz	$\frac{1}{4}$ l; 237 ml
$1\frac{1}{4}$ c	10 oz	3 dl; 296 ml
2 c; 1 pt	16 oz	$\frac{1}{2}$ l; 473 ml
$2\frac{1}{2}$ c	20 oz	592 ml
3 c	24 oz	710 ml; $\frac{3}{4}$ l
4 c; 1 qt	32 oz	1 l; 946 ml
4 qt; 1 gal	128 oz	$3\frac{3}{4}$ l; 3,785 ml
5 qt		$4\frac{3}{4}$ l
6 qt		$5\frac{3}{4}$ l
8 qt		$7\frac{1}{2}$ l

Conversion formula: To convert liters to quarts, multiply the liters by .95; quarts to liters, multiply the quarts by 1.057.

Weight

American ounces	American pounds	Grams	Kilograms
⅓ oz		10 g	
½ oz		15 g	
1 oz		30 g	
3½ oz		100 g	
4 oz	¼ lb	114 g	
5 oz		140 g	
8 oz	½ lb	227 g	
9 oz		250 g	¼ kg
16 oz	1 lb	450 g	
18 oz	1⅛ lb	500 g	½ kg
32 oz	2 lb	900 g	
36 oz	2¼ lb	1000 g	1 kg
	3 lb	1350 g	1⅓ kg
	4 lb	2800 g	1¾ kg

Conversion formula: To convert ounces into grams, multiply the ounces by 28.35; grams into ounces, multiply the grams by .035.

Temperatures

Fahrenheit	Celsius
32°F*	0°C
60°F	16°C
75°F	24°C
80°F	27°C
95°F	37°C
150°F	65°C
175°F	79°C
212°F**	100°C
250°F	121°C
300°F	149°C
350°F	177°C
400°F	205°C
450°F	232°C
500°F	260°C

* water freezes

** water boils

Conversion formula: To convert Fahrenheit into Celsius, subtract 32, multiply by 5, divide by 9. To convert Celsius to Fahrenheit, multiply by 9, divide by 5, add 32.

From Rosenthal, Sylvia, and Fran Shinagee. *How Cooking Works.* New York: Macmillan, 1981.

2

THE NEW YEAR

JANUARY 1

The celebration of the New Year has been called "the grandfather of all other festivals." Throughout the world, peoples—even many regarded as primitive—have kept calendars marking the annual cycle of seasons. The beginning of the year for these peoples is widely marked by ceremonies of some kind. Some scholars regard the excitement of modern New Year's parties as a survival of ancient celebrations reflecting the chaos of an old world ending and a new world beginning. The blowing of party horns, ringing of bells, and cheering are thought to hark back to a time when celebrants tried to scare off evil spirits. The very act of gathering together on this occasion is reminiscent of age-old religious rites performed by a community.

Food plays an important role in most New Year's celebrations. Writing about New Year's in cosmopolitan New York, Fred Ferretti of the *New York Times* has observed: "It is Czech roast goose and French champagne, German venison and plum brandy, Italian baked eel and red wine, Scandinavian baked codfish and Cognac punch, Cuban roast pig and Hungarian red wine, usually separate, occasionally together or in combination, all reflecting the diverse ethnic character of the city and its environs."

It is fitting that desserts rank high among New Year foods. A dessert is by its nature a joyful food. It is the proper finish to a festive meal. And it can be served by itself as a refreshment or snack.

The following assortment of New Year desserts spans eras, countries, and cultures. You will find here Coventry godcakes, said to be given on New Year's Day "from time immemorial" to children by their godparents along with a blessing. There is olie-bollen, a kind of doughnut from Holland that became a favorite in eighteenth-century New York. And note the more exotic novo-godísni pastićki, Bulgarian New Year's cookies. These and the others will grace any New Year's party or reception for family, neighbors, and friends.

Oliebollen—Dutch Fried Puffs

(OH-lee-bow-len)

Dutch settlers brought this New Year's dessert to eighteenth-century New York. Light and crisp, oliebollen have never ceased to be a favorite. *Yields 5 dozen*

> *¾ cup milk*
> *½ cup granulated sugar*
> *½ stick butter*
> *2 eggs*
> *1 tablespoon baking powder*
> *½ teaspoon salt*
> *1 teaspoon ground mace*
> *2¾ cups flour*
> *½ cup dark raisins*
> *vegetable oil for frying*
> *⅓ cup granulated sugar for sprinkling on top*
> *1 teaspoon ground cinnamon for sprinkling on top*
>
> *deep fryer or other deep pan for frying*

1. In a mixing bowl, combine milk, sugar, butter, eggs, baking powder, salt, and mace. Mix. Gradually add flour and raisins.
2. Heat oil to 375°F. Drop spoonfuls of dough into oil. Fry 3 to 4 minutes, or until golden brown, turning over once. Drain on paper towels.
3. Mix sugar and cinnamon. Sprinkle on puffs.

Sneeuwballen—Dutch Snowballs

(snew-BALL-en)

On New Year's Eve, Dutch families eat a late feast. A favorite among the desserts at this meal are these fried cakes with currants in them and a coating of confectioners' sugar. *Yields 5 dozen*

> 1 cup water
> ¼ teaspoon salt
> 1 stick butter
> 2¾ cups all-purpose flour
> 3 eggs
> ¼ cup currants
> ¼ cup finely chopped citron
> 1 tablespoon rum
> vegetable oil for frying
> confectioners' sugar for coating
>
> deep fryer or other deep pan for frying

1. In a saucepan, combine water, salt, and butter. Bring to a boil. Gradually add flour, reserving 2 tablespoons.
2. Add eggs 1 at a time, beating after each addition. Beat until smooth. Mix reserved flour with currants and citron. Add currant mixture and rum. Mix thoroughly.
3. Heat oil to 375°F. Drop batter, roughly shaped into a ball, into oil. Turning once, fry a few at a time until golden brown. Drain on paper towels. Cool. Put confectioners' sugar in a lunch-size paper bag. Shake a few snowballs at a time until fully coated.

NOTE: You may have to coat snowballs again with confectioners' sugar before serving.

Appelbeignets—Dutch Apple Fritters

(AP-ple-ben-yays)

Along with making a racket to drive away evil spirits, the Dutch celebrate New Year's Eve by serving delicacies such as these tasty apple fritters. Eat them while they're still hot! *Yields 16*

⅔ cup all-purpose flour
½ teaspoon baking powder
⅛ teaspoon salt
⅔ cup milk
4 cooking apples
vegetable oil for deep frying
confectioners' sugar for sprinkling on top

deep fryer or frying pan

1. In a mixing bowl, combine flour, baking powder, and salt. Add milk and stir until smooth.
2. Peel and core apples. Cut them into 4 rings each. Heat deep fat to 375°F. Dip rings in batter. Fry several rings at a time about 2 minutes on each side, or until golden brown.
3. Remove fritters and drain on paper towels. Sprinkle freely with confectioners' sugar and serve *immediately*.

Koekjes—Dutch New Year's Cookies

(KOOK-ees)

The Dutch in New York traditionally served these cookies on New Year's Eve. A plain cookie with caraway seeds, it has a flavor that never palls. According to Washington Irving, the Dutch stamped the features of Rip Van Winkle on one side. You can shape them as you will. *Yields about 5 dozen small cookies*

> 3¼ cups all-purpose flour
> ½ tablespoon baking powder
> ¼ teaspoon salt
> 1 teaspoon ground nutmeg
> 2 eggs
> ¾ cup granulated sugar
> ¾ cup sour cream
> 2 tablespoons caraway seeds
> granulated sugar for sprinkling on top
>
> small cookie cutters; baking sheet

1. In a small bowl, combine flour, baking powder, salt, and nutmeg. Set aside.

2. In a mixing bowl, beat eggs and sugar together until light and fluffy. Add sour cream and caraway seeds and gradually the dry ingredients. Mix thoroughly.

3. Refrigerate overnight. On a lightly floured surface, roll out dough to ⅛-inch thickness. Cut with small cookie cutters. Place on lightly greased baking sheet.

4. Bake in a preheated 350°F oven 10 to 15 minutes, or until light brown. Cool on a wire rack. Sprinkle freely with sugar.

Coventry Godcakes

These delicate mincemeat tarts are an ancient New Year's tradition around Coventry, England—especially as a gift from godparents to their godchildren. *Yields about 2–2½ dozen*

> 1 *pound butter*
> 4 *cups all-purpose flour*
> 1 *teaspoon salt*
> 1⅓–1½ *cups ice water*

> **Filling** *(if preferred, use prepared mincemeat)*
> 6 *tablespoons butter*
> ½ *cup light brown sugar, firmly packed*
> 1 *teaspoon ground cinnamon*
> ½ *teaspoon ground nutmeg*
> ½ *teaspoon ground allspice*
> ½ *cup currants*
> ⅓ *cup lemon peel, finely chopped*
> ⅓ *cup candied orange peel, finely chopped*

> *baking sheet*

1. In a mixing bowl, mix butter and ¼ cup of the flour. Place between two sheets of wax paper and flatten into an 8-inch square. Refrigerate at least 30 minutes.

2. In a mixing bowl, combine remaining flour and salt. Add cold water until a pliable paste forms that is neither sticky nor dry.

3. On a lightly floured board, knead dough until smooth and elastic. Roll out to 9 by 17 inches. Take butter mixture from refrigerator and peel off one sheet of wax paper. Butter side down, cover ½ of dough. Remove other sheet of wax paper.

4. Fold dough over butter mixture. Pinch edges tightly together. Roll out dough to 9 by 17 inches. Fold in thirds. Roll out

and fold in thirds two more times. *Refrigerate while making filling.*

5. In a mixing bowl, cream butter and sugar until light and fluffy. Add remaining ingredients. Mix well.

6. Roll out to ⅛-inch thickness. Cut into 3-inch squares. Put filling in center of each square. Moisten edges. Fold dough in half to form triangles. Seal edges with a fork.

7. Place on ungreased baking sheet. Bake in a preheated 425°F oven 12 to 15 minutes, or until golden brown. Cool on a wire rack.

Black Bun—Scottish New Year's Eve Cake

Black bun is traditional for Hogmanay, the Scottish New Year's Eve. Sample this delicately crusted, spicy cake, and you'll know why the Scots love it. (Make it early to allow time for aging.) *Yields 1 cake*

Crust
2½ cups flour
1 teaspoon baking powder
½ teaspoon salt
1 stick butter
1 egg
3–5 tablespoons ice water

Cake
2 cups all-purpose flour
1 cup currants
2 cups muscat raisins
1 cup blanched almonds, coarsely chopped
1 cup mixed candied fruit peel
½ tablespoon ground cinnamon
½ teaspoon ground ginger

½ *teaspoon ground cloves*
½ *teaspoon black pepper*
½ *teaspoon baking soda*
1 *cup milk*
3 *tablespoons brandy*
1 *egg, beaten, for glaze*

9 × 5 × 3-inch loaf pan

1. To make crust: In a mixing bowl, combine flour, baking powder, and salt. Cut in butter with two knives or a pastry blender until mixture looks like coarse meal.

2. Add egg and gradually the cold water 1 tablespoon at a time, tossing with a fork after each addition. Continue until dough can be gathered into a ball. Wrap ball in foil or plastic wrap. Chill.

3. To make cake: In a mixing bowl, combine ¼ cup of the flour, currants, raisins, almonds, and candied fruit peel. Toss. Add spices, pepper, baking soda, and remaining flour.

4. Gradually add milk and brandy. Mix thoroughly. Set aside.

5. Cut off ⅓ of crust and set aside. Roll the crust out sufficiently to cover bottom and sides of loaf pan. Place in greased loaf pan. Put cake filling inside crust.

6. Roll out remaining crust and place over top of cake filling with 1 inch overhang. Seal edges; flute. With a sharp knife, cut slits in top. Brush with beaten egg.

7. Bake in a 250°F oven 3 hours, or until lightly browned. Cool in pan about 10 minutes. Remove and cool completely on a wire rack.

NOTE: To allow proper aging, make 2 weeks ahead of time.

Xerotígana—Greek New Year's Crisps

(zay-ro-TEE-gha-nah)

The Greeks serve these delicate deep-fried pastries, topped with nuts and a honey syrup, to welcome in the New Year. *Yields about 7 dozen*

> 5 *eggs*
> 1 *tablespoon olive oil*
> 3 *tablespoons orange juice*
> 3 *cups all-purpose flour*

> **Honey Syrup**
> 2¾ *cups honey*
> 2 *cups water*
> ⅓ *cup lemon juice*
> 1 *teaspoon ground cinnamon*

> 4 *cups olive oil for deep frying*
> *coarsely chopped walnuts for sprinkling on top*

> *deep fryer or other deep pan for frying*

1. In a mixing bowl, beat eggs until light and foamy. Add olive oil, orange juice, and flour. Mix thoroughly. Cover and set aside 1 hour.

2. To make honey syrup: In a saucepan, combine honey, water, lemon juice, and cinnamon. Boil 5 minutes. Set aside.

3. Roll out dough to ⅛-inch thickness. Using a pastry wheel, cut pieces 1 by 3 inches. Pinch centers to make "butterfly wings."

4. Heat oil to 375°F. Fry a few wings a minute or two until golden brown, turning once. Drain on paper towels. Place a layer of wings on a platter. Spoon some of the honey syrup on wings; sprinkle with a few walnuts. Repeat until all the wings are covered.

NOTE: For best flavor, serve a day after making.

Novogodiśni Pastićki—
Bulgarian New Year's Cookies

(no-vo-go-DEESH-nee PAST-eech-kee)

These butter cookies, traditional on New Year's Eve in Bulgaria, are an elegant treat. Their delicate flavor always pleases. *Yields 2–3 dozen*

> 3 sticks butter
> 1²/₃ cups confectioners' sugar
> 4 eggs
> 1²/₃ cups flour
> 1 tablespoon ground cinnamon
> ½ cup blanched almonds, finely ground
> 2 tablespoons granulated sugar
>
> 13 × 9-inch pan

1. In a mixing bowl, cream butter and sugar until light and fluffy. Add eggs 1 at a time, beating after each addition. Add flour and 2 teaspoons of the cinnamon. Mix.

2. Spread in greased baking pans. Bake in a preheated 350°F oven 30 to 40 minutes, or until a cake tester comes out clean.

3. While baking, combine in a small bowl the remaining cinnamon, almonds, and sugar. Mix. Sprinkle on top of baked cookies. Cut into squares while still warm.

3

TWELFTH NIGHT

(EPIPHANY)

JANUARY 6

Falling twelve days after Christmas, Twelfth Night traditionally concludes the Christmas season. People have long marked the occasion with parties and merrymaking. But as Epiphany, the festival carries deep religious overtones. In religious terms this refers to the baptism of Jesus and the coming of the three Magi— the first manifestation of Jesus to the Gentiles. Sometimes the adoration of the Magi is presented as a pageant in church.

But revelry is the keynote of traditional Twelfth Night feasts. These are typically hearty meals, with rounds of roast beef and ideally a garnished boar's head served in a room or hall decked with Christmas ornaments. A Twelfth Night cake with a pea, bean, coin, or figurine in it often completes the meal. A lucky man who finds a dried bean in his piece of cake becomes king of the festivities or a lucky woman who finds a dried bean or pea becomes queen. The king or queen chooses a consort and leads the group in games and other diversions.

Other desserts are also traditional at Twelfth Night feasts. They'll help to make your Twelfth Night party a hit of the Christmas season.

Twelfth Night Pound Cake

This is a rich plain cake for those who don't want too sweet a dessert. Purists will bake it in a Turk's-head mold, but a Bundt pan will do. *Yields 1 cake*

> 1 *pound butter*
> 1½ *cups granulated sugar*
> 8 *eggs*
> 2 *tablespoons brandy*
> 4 *cups all-purpose flour*
> ½ *teaspoon salt*
> ½ *tablespoon baking powder*
> ½ *tablespoon ground mace*
> *brandy for soaking cake*
> *confectioners' sugar for sprinkling on top*
>
> *Turk's-head mold pan; cheesecloth*

1. In a mixing bowl, combine butter and sugar until light and fluffy. Add eggs 1 at a time, beating after each addition. Add brandy.

2. In a mixing bowl, combine flour, salt, baking powder, and mace. Add ½ cup at a time to butter mixture. Mix.

3. Pour into greased and lightly floured mold pan. Bake in a 300°F oven 2 hours, or until a cake tester comes out clean. Leave in pan 15 minutes; then cool on a wire rack.

4. Wrap in cheesecloth. Soak with brandy, and keep cloth damp.

NOTES: To serve, sprinkle lightly with confectioners' sugar. Cut into thin slices.

Make 2 or 3 weeks before using.

Galette des Rois—Kings' Cake

(ga-LET day RWA)

In France, Twelfth Night is greeted with joyful customs that often vary from province to province. But one especially widespread tradition is the serving of a cake such as the one here. This cake may contain a dry bean, the finder of which becomes king or queen of the Twelfth Night party with the right to choose a corresponding queen or king. *Yields 1 cake*

> 2 cups all-purpose flour
> ½ teaspoon baking soda
> 1 teaspoon ground cinnamon
> ½ teaspoon ground cloves
> ½ teaspoon ground nutmeg
> ½ teaspoon ground allspice
> ¼ teaspoon ground mace
> 1 stick butter
> 1¾ cups light brown sugar, firmly packed
> 2 eggs
> 1 cup milk
> 1 tablespoon lemon juice
>
> *10-inch tube pan*

1. In a bowl, combine flour, baking soda, and spices. Mix. Set aside.

2. In a mixing bowl, cream butter and sugar until light and fluffy. Add eggs. Mix. Combine milk and lemon juice in a cup. Set aside.

3. Gradually add milk to butter mixture, alternating with flour mixture.

4. Grease and flour cake pan. Pour batter into pan. Bake in a preheated 350°F oven 50 to 60 minutes, or until a cake tester comes out clean. Cool in pan 10 minutes. Remove from pan and cool on a wire rack.

English Twelfth Night Cake I

Another treat for a Twelfth Night celebration, this one is richer and heartier than the pound cake. Few people can resist the candied fruit and spices that make this such a delicious finish to the Christmas season. *Yields 12-inch round cake*

>   ¼ *cup dry sherry, rum, or brandy*
>   ½ *cup golden raisins*
>   ½ *cup currants*
>   2 *cups mixed candied fruit peel, finely chopped*
>   ½ *cup candied cherries, cut in half*
>   ½ *cup diced candied orange peel*
>   3 *cups all-purpose flour*
>   ½ *teaspoon baking powder*
>   1 *teaspoon ground cinnamon*
>   ½ *teaspoon ground mace*
>   ½ *teaspoon ground allspice*
>   1 *teaspoon grated orange peel*
>   ½ *cup slivered blanched almonds, coarsely chopped*
>   2 *sticks butter*
>   ¾ *dark brown sugar, firmly packed*
>   4 *eggs*
>
>   *12-inch springform pan*

1. In a large bowl, combine sherry, raisins, currants, fruit peel, cherries, and orange peel. Set aside 1 hour.

2. In a small bowl, combine 2½ cups of the flour, baking powder, spices, orange peel and almonds. Set aside.

3. In a mixing bowl, cream butter and sugar until light and fluffy. Add eggs 1 at a time, beating after each addition. Gradually add dry ingredients from small bowl. Mix thoroughly.

4. Sprinkle remaining flour on the ingredients in the large bowl, tossing to coat pieces of fruit evenly. Fold the fruit mixture into the cake batter.

5. Grease cake pan with butter. Lightly coat with flour and shake out excess. Pour batter into the prepared pan.

6. Bake in a preheated 350°F oven about 1½ hours, or until a cake tester comes out clean. Cool cake in pan about 30 minutes. Then remove sides of the pan and cool completely on a wire rack.

NOTE: To allow cake to mellow, wait at least a day after baking before cutting.

English Twelfth Night Cake II

Here's a second Twelfth Night cake traditional in England for centuries. It lacks the candied fruit of the other cake and has a delicately dry texture that many people relish. *Yields 1 cake*

> 1 *stick butter*
> ¼ *cup granulated sugar*
> ¾ *cup all-purpose flour*
> 1 *teaspoon ground nutmeg*
> ½ *teaspoon ground cinnamon*
> ½ *teaspoon ground ginger*
> 2 *teaspoons baking soda*
> 2½ *cups heavy cream*
> 1 *cup currants*
> 1 *dried pea (optional)*
> 1 *dried bean (optional)*
>
> **Topping**
> 1 *cup granulated sugar*
> 2 *tablespoons rosewater*
>
> *8-inch springform pan;*
> *ovenproof dish large enough to hold cake*

1. In a mixing bowl, cream butter and sugar until light and fluffy. In another bowl, combine flour and spices. Set aside.

2. In a small saucepan, heat baking soda and ½ cup of the cream to warm. Combine butter mixture, flour mixture, warm cream, and remaining cream. Mix thoroughly. Add currants and, if desired, dried pea and bean. Mix.

3. Pour batter into greased baking pan. Bake in a preheated 350°F oven 1¼ hours, or until a cake tester comes out clean. Remove from pan and place on a wire rack 15 minutes.

4. In a small saucepan, bring sugar and rosewater to a boil. After cake has cooled 15 minutes, place upside down in ovenproof dish. Spoon sugar-and-rosewater mixture on top. Lower heat of oven to 325°F and bake 15 minutes more. Cool on a wire rack.

4

VALENTINE'S DAY

FEBRUARY 14

How did Valentine's Day begin? Historians debate this question, relying on legends and even legends of legends to attempt an answer. Ancient Rome may have provided the germ of the holiday with a spring festival called Lupercalia, celebrated on February 15 and intended to ensure the fertility of people, animals, and fields. The Christian Church abolished Lupercalia in 495 A.D., and Pope Gelasius replaced the pagan holiday the following year with Saint Valentine's Day.

Saint Valentine is an obscure martyr, or rather Saint Valentines *are*, since there are two saints of that name. Both were reputed to have been killed on February 14. The legends surrounding the compound Saint Valentine were probably influenced by Lupercalia and the proximity of the date to spring. It came to be widely held that February 14 was a good day to choose a mate. In *A Midsummer Night's Dream,* Shakespeare wrote, "St. Valentine is past; / Begin these woodbirds but to couple now?"

In the 1700's, English maidens were following various customs on this day, such as drawing names out of a jar, to foretell who would be their future husband. Lovers used the holiday as an occasion to exchange love letters and tokens of affection. Valentine cards became widespread in the nineteenth century. But at least a large minority of people in the Western world have long presented sweethearts with various other expressions of tenderness such as boxes of candy, flowers, fruit, and articles of clothing.

Desserts are still another Valentine's Day offering, especially appropriate because of their sweetness. Why not try these Valentine desserts for a less usual but traditional gift to the Valentine(s) of your choice?

Austrian Valentine Cookies

These heart-shaped cookies, laced with ginger and molasses, are an Austrian tradition that will delight your Valentine. Decorations with icing make the cookies as attractive to look at as they are good to eat. *Yields about 3½ dozen 3-inch heart-shaped cookies*

2 *sticks butter*
⅓ *cup granulated sugar*
4 *cups all-purpose flour*
½ *teaspoon ground cloves*
½ *teaspoon ground mace*
⅔ *cup dark molasses*

Icing
1 *cup sifted confectioners' sugar*
1 *teaspoon vanilla extract*
2 *tablespoons water*

3-inch heart-shaped cookie cutter; baking sheet

1. In a mixing bowl, cream butter and sugar until light and fluffy. Gradually add dry ingredients and molasses. Mix thoroughly. Chill at least 2 hours.
2. On a lightly floured surface, roll out dough to ⅛-inch thickness. Using heart-shaped cookie cutter, cut out cookies. Place on greased baking sheet. Bake in a preheated 350°F oven 8 to 10 minutes, or until golden brown. Cool on a wire rack.
3. Combine icing ingredients. Mix thoroughly. Decorate cookies with icing.

NOTE: Store in an airtight container.

Szerelmes Levél—Hungarian Love Letters

(ser-el-em le-VEL)

These cookies, folded to look like envelopes, contain a delicious Valentine's Day "message"—an orange-walnut filling. They're excellent as well for any sentimental occasion such as an engagement party. *Yields about 2–2½ dozen 3-inch-square cookies*

> 2 sticks butter
> ¼ cup granulated sugar
> ⅛ teaspoon salt
> ½ teaspoon grated orange peel
> ⅔ cup sour cream
> 2¾ cups all-purpose flour

Filling
> 1 tablespoon grated orange peel
> ¾ cup finely chopped walnuts

Topping
> 2 egg whites, beaten
> sugar for sprinkling on top

> baking sheet

1. In a mixing bowl, cream butter and sugar until light and fluffy. Add salt, orange peel, sour cream, and gradually the flour. Mix thoroughly. Chill overnight.

2. In a small bowl, combine orange peel and walnuts. Mix. On a lightly floured surface, roll out dough to ⅛-inch thickness. Cut into 3-inch squares.

3. Place 1 teaspoon of filling in center of each cookie. Fold each pair of diagonally opposite ends to center.

4. Place on ungreased baking sheet. Brush with beaten egg whites. Sprinkle tops with sugar.

5. Bake in a preheated 350°F oven 20 to 25 minutes, or until golden brown. Cool on a wire rack.

Valentine Cake

What could say "Happy Valentine's Day" more expressively than a heart-shaped cake? If you don't have two heart-shaped pans, the directions explain how to make a heart using a round and a square pan. *Yields 1*

> 2 cups all-purpose flour
> 3 teaspoons baking powder
> 1/2 teaspoon salt
> 1 stick butter
> 1 1/4 cups granulated sugar
> 1 cup milk
> 1 teaspoon almond extract
> 4 egg whites

Icing
> 2/3 cup granulated sugar
> 1/2 teaspoon cream of tartar
> 1/8 teaspoon salt
> 2 egg whites
> 1/3 cup cold water
> 1 teaspoon almond extract
> few drops red food coloring
> red cinnamon candies for decoration (optional)

> 2 8-inch heart-shaped pans; double boiler (see note).

1. In a small bowl, combine flour, baking powder, and salt. In a mixing bowl, cream butter and sugar until light and fluffy.

2. Gradually add flour mixture and milk alternately to mixing bowl. Add almond extract.

3. In another bowl, beat egg whites until stiff peaks stand up. Gently fold egg whites into batter.

4. Pour into greased and floured cake pans. Bake in a preheated 350°F oven 20 to 25 minutes, or until a cake tester comes out clean. Cool in pan about 10 minutes, then cool on a wire rack.

5. To make icing: In the top of a double boiler, combine sugar, cream of tartar, salt, egg whites, and cold water. Place over hot, but not boiling, water at low heat.

6. Beat constantly with an electric or rotary beater until icing stands in stiff peaks, about 7 minutes. Remove from heat.

7. Beat in almond extract and food coloring (just enough to make frosting a delicate pink).

8. If cake has been baked in round and square pans, cut round layer in half. Place semicircles on adjacent sides of square to form heart.

9. Ice the cake. If desired, use cinnamon candies to decorate.

NOTE: If you don't have heart-shaped pans, use one 8-inch round pan and one 8-inch square pan for a one-layer cake, or two 8-inch round pans and two 8-inch square pans for a two-layer cake, doubling the recipe.

5

WASHINGTON'S BIRTHDAY

THIRD MONDAY IN FEBRUARY

For more than two centuries, Americans have been enthusiastically celebrating George Washington's birthday. In the early days of the Republic, ships fired thirteen-gun salutes and revelers flocked to balls and parties at inns, mansions, and ordinary homes, where they dined on oysters, hams, and turkeys. They quaffed wine and punch, typically offering a toast to each state of the Union in turn. The *pièce de résistance* was often a magnificent cake decorated with sugar ornaments and fruits.

President Washington himself, though he shunned personal adulation, participated in a formal celebration of his birthday in 1795 held in Philadelphia, the nation's capital during the 1790's. A witness tells how President and Mrs. Washington cordially greeted the guests and invited them into an adjoining room for wine and cake. "The cake was round and nearly three feet in diameter and one in thickness," the witness recalled. "His wine was excellent and his punch high flavored. We all joined in the conviviality, the President mingling and partaking with the company." That night the Washingtons attended a birthday ball in his honor, an annual event.

On Washington's two-hundred-fiftieth birthday in 1982, Americans celebrated in a colorful variety of ways. A parade, concerts of Colonial music, birthday parties with huge cakes, museum exhibitions, and cherry-pie eating contests marked the occasion. At a children's party in the Morris-Jumel Mansion in New York City, once General Washington's headquarters, children dressed in colonial costumes sang "Happy Birthday to George" and blew out two hundred fifty candles on a cherry-topped cake.

Note the cherries. That tradition is based on the story that young George confessed to having chopped down a cherry tree. Although apocryphal, of course, the legend has given rise to some delightful desserts.

Cherry Pie

It is mere legend that young George Washington confessed after chopping down a cherry tree. But cherries, and especially cherry pie, are firmly associated in the United States with Washington's Birthday. This recipe makes a pie fit for the Father of Our Country. *Yields 1 pie*

> *(For pie crust ingredients see page 4.)*
> *4 cups canned pitted tart cherries*
> *2 tablespoons quick-cooking tapioca*
> *1⅓ cups granulated sugar*
> *⅛ teaspoon salt*
> *½ teaspoon almond extract*
> *1 tablespoon butter*
>
> *9-inch pie plate*

(For pie crust preparation see page 4. Reserve ⅓ of pie crust.)

1. Drain cherries and reserve ½ cup of the juice. In a bowl, combine cherries, juice, tapioca, sugar, salt, and almond extract. Stir. Set aside 15 minutes.

2. Put cherry filling in pie plate. Dot with butter. Roll out remaining dough ⅛ inch thick and ½ inch wide. Place strips across top of pie, then interweave other strips to form a lattice. Trim edges of lattice, seal, and crimp.

3. Bake in a preheated 450°F oven 15 minutes. Lower heat to 400°F and bake 30 to 40 minutes.

George Washington Cake

This recipe, adapted from one dated 1780 and bearing George Washington's name, comes from an old Williamsburg, Virginia family cookbook. *Yields 1 cake*

> 1 *pound butter*
> 1½ *cups granulated sugar*
> 4 *eggs, separated*
> 4 *cups flour*
> ½ *tablespoon ground mace*
> 1 *tablespoon baking powder*
> 1 *cup milk*
> ½ *cup dark raisins*
> ¼ *cup currants*
> ¼ *cup finely chopped citron*

> **Icing**
> 3 *cups confectioners' sugar*
> 2 *tablespoons butter*
> 5–6 *tablespoons water*
> 1 *teaspoon almond extract*

> *10-inch tube pan*

1. In a mixing bowl, cream butter and sugar until light and fluffy. Add egg yolks and stir.
2. In another bowl, combine flour, mace, and baking powder. Gradually add flour mixture and milk alternately. Stir in raisins, currants, and citron.
3. Beat egg whites until stiff peaks stand up. Fold into batter. Pour into greased and lightly floured tube pan. Bake in a preheated 350°F oven 50 to 60 minutes, or until a cake tester comes out clean. Cool on a wire rack.
4. To make icing: Combine confectioners' sugar, butter, and water. Mix thoroughly. Add almond extract. Ice cooled cake.

6

CARNIVAL AND LENT

Easter, the celebration of Christ's resurrection and the chief Christian feast, is preceded by Carnival and Lent. The forty-day Lenten period features a somber array of holy days filled with traditions that remind Christians of the Passion of Christ and their religious commitments.

Carnival

Carnival is a time of merrymaking and feasting carried on in a mood of abandon before Lent. *Carnival* literally means "the putting away of flesh," a reference to the tradition of giving up meat during the Lenten season. In the Roman Catholic countries of Europe, carnival was a colorful and often raucous celebration. Masked and costumed participants danced in the streets, played pranks, and flirted. They drank deeply and ate freely of the foods they would soon deny themselves.

Shrove Tuesday

Originally, Carnival lasted several weeks from January 6 (Epiphany) to the first day of Lent (Ash Wednesday). This period was shortened to three days ending in Shrove Tuesday. The latter day received its name because it was observed by *shriving*—confessing sins and receiving forgiveness for them. The faithful doing so were considered shriven, or *shrove*.

One ancient tradition on Shrove Tuesday is to cook pancakes and thus use up fats forbidden during Lent, giving rise to the alternate name of Pancake Day. A Shrove Tuesday pancake race has taken place in Olney, England, for more than five hundred years. Women contestants run 415 yards to the church door with a fry pan in which a pancake is cooking. This pancake must be flipped three times during the race. The winner receives a kiss from the bell ringer and a prayer book; the runner-up a prayer book. Several other towns in England and the United States have a similar tradition.

In the United States, the most famous Shrove Tuesday celebration is the Mardi Gras in New Orleans—marked by parties, masked balls, and a grand parade.

Mothering Sunday

Mothering Sunday, or Laetare Sunday, falls in the middle of Lent —the fourth Sunday. *Mothering* has a theological origin, perhaps referring to a traditional visit on this day to the cathedral, or mother church. Common practice sometimes altered that tradition to visiting one's mother.

Holy Week

The last week of Lent, Holy Week, commemorates the last days of Christ's life. Included are the following sacred observances:

Palm Sunday: The Sunday before Easter, it recalls Christ's entry into Jerusalem. Churchgoers receive palm branches in memory of those strewn before Christ as he entered the city. This day is sometimes called Fig Sunday because of the barren fig tree along the way that Christ caused to wither.

Good Friday: Commemorating Christ's crucifixion, this is the most somber of all the holy days. Throughout Christendom, church services are held from noon to three o'clock, the time when Christ hung on the cross.

Holy Saturday: On this day, Christ rested in the tomb. The faithful ready themselves for Easter, traditionally lighting Easter candles for their homes from a large paschal candle in each church.

Fastnachtküchlein—Swiss Carnival Cookies

(FAHST-nakt-KOOK-line)

These cookies, fried to a golden brown and very crisp, are a favorite in Switzerland during Carnival. Light and delicious. *Yields about 2 dozen*

> 2 eggs
> 3 tablespoons heavy cream
> ¼ teaspoon salt
> 3 tablespoons granulated sugar
> 2 cups all-purpose flour
> vegetable oil for frying
> confectioners' sugar for sprinkling on top
>
> deep fryer or other deep pan for frying

1. In a mixing bowl, combine eggs, cream, salt, and sugar. Mix together. Gradually add flour. Mix.
2. On a lightly floured surface, knead dough 5 minutes. Cover with an inverted bowl 30 minutes. Cut dough into walnut-size pieces. On a lightly floured surface, roll out dough as thin as possible. Each should be a circle roughly about 5 inches in diameter. Put aside to dry 15 minutes.
3. While circles are resting, preheat deep fat to 375°F, or until the fat can brown a 1-inch cube of bread in 60 seconds. Fry 5 minutes, or until golden brown, turning once. Drain on paper towels. (They should have a crumpled appearance.) Sprinkle with confectioners' sugar.

NOTE: Store in an airtight container.

Greek Sweet Puffs

Served in Greece just before Lent, these deep-fried pastries dipped in syrup are so light and tasty you'll have to force yourself to stop eating them. *Yields 3 dozen*

Syrup
1²/₃ *cups granulated sugar*
1¹/₃ *cups water*
1 *teaspoon grated lemon rind*
6 *whole cloves*
1 *cinnamon stick, broken in half*
³/₄ *cup honey*
2 *tablespoons lemon juice*
2 *tablespoons brandy*

Dough
³/₄ *cup water*
¹/₂ *stick butter*
1 *teaspoon ground cinnamon*
¹/₂ *teaspoon salt*
³/₄ *cup all-purpose flour*
2 *eggs*
vegetable oil for frying

Topping
¹/₃ *cup ground walnuts*
¹/₃ *cup confectioners' sugar*
¹/₂ *tablespoon ground cinnamon*

deep fryer or other deep pan for frying

1. To make syrup: In a saucepan, combine sugar, water, lemon rind, cloves, and cinnamon pieces. Bring to a boil, stirring constantly until slightly thick.

2. Remove from heat. Add honey, lemon juice, and brandy. Cool. Just before using, remove cloves and cinnamon pieces.

3. To make puffs: In a saucepan, combine water, butter, cinnamon, and salt. Boil 2 minutes. Add flour, stirring vigorously. Cook until mixture thickens and pulls away from the side of the pan. Cool.

4. Add eggs 1 at a time, beating after each addition. Heat oil to 375°F. Drop spoonfuls of dough into oil. Fry 3 to 4 minutes, or until golden brown, turning over once. Drain on paper towels.

5. Dip each puff into syrup and place on a serving dish. Sprinkle walnuts, sugar, and cinnamon on top of puffs.

NOTE: Best when served hot.

Crème Brûlée

(CREM broo-LAY)

This glazed custard is a tradition in New Orleans the night before Mardi Gras. It's an ideal dessert—with simple ingredients and a complex flavor. (Make early in the morning or even the night before.) *Yields 4–6 servings*

> 4 *eggs*
> 1/3 *cup dark brown sugar, firmly packed*
> 1/2 *teaspoon salt*
> 2 *cups heavy cream, hot*
> *dark brown sugar for sprinkling on top*
>
> *pie plate*

1. In a saucepan, combine eggs, brown sugar, and salt. Slowly add cream. Beat until smooth.

2. Cook 5 to 7 minutes, stirring constantly. Strain. Let cool to room temperature. To prevent film from forming on the surface,

stir occasionally. After pudding has cooled, cover and refrigerate 4 to 6 hours.

3. To make glaze: Sprinkle brown sugar evenly on top of custard. Set under preheated broiler, leaving door open, until sugar melts. Serve promptly or chill an hour or two before serving.

NOTE: The crust of *crème brûlée* is crackly or hard.

Mardi Gras Fudge

The Shrove Tuesday celebration in New Orleans, Mardi Gras, is world-famed for its exuberant and colorful parades. Not so well known, but worthy of note, are several delicacies traditionally served in the city on this festive occasion. This extraordinary cherry- and pecan-studded fudge is one. Connoisseurs place it in the first rank of gourmet fudge. *Yields 64 1–inch square pieces*

> ½ stick butter
> 12 ounces semisweet chocolate bits
> 12-ounce can sweet condensed milk
> 1 teaspoon almond extract
> ⅛ teaspoon salt
> 2 tablespoons chopped golden raisins
> ⅓ cup chopped candied cherries
> ⅓ cup coarsely chopped pecans

> 8 × 8-inch pan

1. In a double boiler, melt butter and chocolate, stirring constantly. Add milk, almond extract, and salt. Stir until smooth.

2. Stir in raisins, cherries, and pecans. Place in greased pan. Refrigerate until firm. (Can be made up to 3 days before serving.)

Shrove Tuesday Knots

These crisp deep-fried pastries mean Shrove Tuesday in the Tuscany region of Italy. Try them as they are or with whipped cream. *Yields about 3½ dozen*

> 2¾ cups all-purpose flour
> ½ cup granulated sugar
> ⅛ teaspoon salt
> ½ tablespoon baking powder
> 3 tablespoons butter
> 2 eggs
> 2 tablespoons brandy
> vegetable oil for deep frying
> confectioners' sugar for sprinkling on top
>
> deep fryer

1. In a bowl, combine flour, sugar, salt, and baking powder. Set aside. In a mixing bowl, combine butter, eggs, and brandy. Gradually add dry ingredients. Mix thoroughly. Shape into a ball and chill overnight.

2. On a floured surface, roll out dough to ⅛-inch thickness. Cut into strips ¾ inch thick and 7 inches long. Tie each into a knot.

3. Heat oil to 375°F. Place knots in oil, 4 or 5 at a time. When golden brown, turn over. Drain on paper towels. While hot, sprinkle with confectioners' sugar. Sprinkle again when about to serve.

NOTE: Store in an airtight container.

Crowdie Cream

This oatmeal-and-rum dessert is a tradition in Scotland on Shrove Tuesday. In it, the tang of rum blends most agreeably with the smoothness of heavy cream—the whole textured with that most Scottish of grains, oatmeal. Sometimes a ring was hidden in this dessert, with the finder assured of being married within the year. *Yields 4–6 servings*

½ cup regular oatmeal
1⅓ cups heavy cream
¼ cup confectioners' sugar
2 tablespoons dark rum

baking sheet

1. Spread oatmeal evenly on the bottom of baking sheet. Toast in a preheated 350°F oven 5 to 10 minutes, or until golden brown. Allow to cool.

2. Whip cream until it starts to thicken. Gradually add sugar and wait until stiff peaks stand up.

3. Stir in rum, a little at a time. Fold in toasted oatmeal. Serve at once.

Shrove Tuesday Pancakes

Because of the Shrove Tuesday tradition of serving pancakes, this day came to be known also as Pancake Day. These pancakes, served with lemon juice and confectioners' sugar, are a delicious way to celebrate the holiday. *Yields 1½ dozen*

> 1⅔ cups all-purpose flour
> ⅛ teaspoon salt
> 1 tablespoon granulated sugar
> 2 eggs
> ¾ cup milk
> ¾ cup water
> 1 tablespoon grated lemon rind
> 1 tablespoon melted butter
> oil for frying
> lemon juice for sprinkling on top
> confectioners' sugar for sprinkling on top
>
> griddle or a fry pan

1. In a bowl, combine flour, salt, and sugar. Mix and set aside. In a mixing bowl, beat eggs until light and fluffy.
2. Gradually add flour mixture, milk, water, and lemon rind. Mix until batter is fairly smooth. Cover and refrigerate about 1 hour.
3. Add melted butter to batter. Grease heated griddle or fry pan lightly. To make thin pancakes, pour batter a little at a time into pan. Turn each pancake over once when bubbles cover top.
4. Serve pancakes hot, covered lightly with lemon juice and confectioners' sugar.

Lenten Pie

This pie, similar to a Christmas mince pie, is a lighter version, without candied fruit. Yet the pie has a true mince flavor that makes it a real treat. *Yields 2 pies*

> 2 *unbaked pie shells*
> 3 *pounds apples, peeled, cored, and coarsely chopped*
> 1 *cup currants*
> 1 *cup dark raisins*
> 4 *hard-boiled eggs, finely chopped*
> 1/2 *teaspoon ground cinnamon*
> 1/2 *teaspoon ground cloves*
> 1/2 *teaspoon ground mace*
> 1/2 *teaspoon ground nutmeg*
> 2 *tablespoons lemon juice*
> 1 *teaspoon grated lemon rind*
> 2 *tablespoons orange juice*
> 1 *teaspoon orange rind*
> 1 *cup granulated sugar*
> 1/4 *cup brandy*
> 1/4 *cup sherry*
>
> 2 *pie plates*

1. Make pie crust according to the instructions on page 4. (Reserve 1/3 of pie crust.)

2. In a mixing bowl, combine ingredients. Mix well. Pour into two pie plates.

3. Roll out remaining dough 1/8 inch thick and 1/2 inch wide. Place strips across top of pies, then interweave other strips to form a lattice. Trim edges of lattice, seal, and crimp.

4. Bake in a preheated 375°F oven 40 to 50 minutes, or until golden brown.

Capirotada—Mexican Bread Pudding

(cah-peer-oh-TAH-da)

A widespread favorite in Mexico during Lent, this delightful pudding has a haunting flavor reminiscent of pineapple—though there is no pineapple in it. Note that cake is used here as an ingredient instead of bread. *Yields 6–8 servings*

> 1¼ *cups water*
> 1½ *cups granulated sugar*
> 1 *teaspoon ground cinnamon*
> 3 *tablespoons butter*
> 3 *eggs, separated,*
> ¼ *cup brandy*
> ¾ *cup golden raisins*
> 14 *thin slices pound cake, homemade or storebought*
> 8 *ounces Monterey Jack cheese*
>
> *8-inch square baking dish*

1. In a saucepan, bring to a boil water, sugar, and cinnamon.
2. Remove from heat. Add butter. Cool slightly. Add egg yolks, brandy, and raisins. Mix thoroughly. Beat egg whites until stiff peaks stand up, and fold in.
3. Grease baking dish. Line bottom with slices of cake. Place cheese on top of cake. Pour half the egg mixture on top of cheese. Place a second layer of cake and a second layer of cheese in the baking dish. Pour in remainder of egg mixture.
4. Bake in a preheated 325°F oven about 30 minutes or until set. Serve warm.

Brandy Snaps

These lacy, fingerlike cookies, filled with whipped cream, are a tradition in England for Mothering Sunday. Try them for an unusual treat everyone loves. *Yields about 3 dozen*

> 1½ sticks butter
> ¾ cup dark brown sugar, firmly packed
> ½ cup dark corn syrup
> 2 tablespoons brandy
> 1¼ cups all-purpose flour
> ½ teaspoon ground ginger

> **Filling**
> 1 cup heavy cream
> 2 tablespoons confectioners' sugar
> 1 tablespoon brandy

> *double boiler; baking sheet; wooden spoon;*
> *pastry bag with plain or rosette tube*

1. In double boiler, heat butter, brown sugar, and corn syrup. Bring to a boil, stirring frequently. Remove from heat. Stir in brandy, flour, and ginger. Mix thoroughly.

2. On lightly greased baking sheet, drop teaspoonfuls of batter about 3 inches apart. Bake in a preheated 350°F oven 10 to 15 minutes. Grease very lightly the handle of wooden spoon.

3. After 1 to 2 minutes, carefully remove cookies from baking sheet. Roll each cookie over spoon handle. Slip cookie off handle and place on a wire rack. If cookies harden before being rolled, place in oven a minute to soften.

4. To make filling: In a chilled bowl, beat cream and confectioners' sugar until stiff peaks stand up. Fold in brandy.

5. Using a pastry bag filled with a plain or a rosette tube, pipe filling into each end of cookies. Serve immediately.

NOTE: Store unfilled cookies in an airtight container.

Palm Cookies

Shaped like palm trees, these butter-and-nut cookies based on a recipe from a 1902 cookbook add a delicious touch to Palm Sunday. (Even not shaped like a palm tree, they're still delicious.) *Yields about 2 dozen*

> 6 *tablespoons butter*
> ⅔ *cup granulated sugar*
> 1 *egg*
> 1⅓ *cups all-purpose flour*
> ½ *tablespoon baking powder*
> ½ *cup finely chopped hickory nuts or walnuts*
> 1 *egg white for brushing top*

Icing
> 1½ *cups confectioners' sugar*
> 1 *teaspoon almond extract*
> 4–5 *tablespoons water*
> *green food coloring (optional)*

> *baking sheet; writing tip; pastry bag*

1. In a mixing bowl, cream butter and sugar until light and fluffy. Add egg, flour, baking powder, and nuts. Mix thoroughly. Chill 1 hour.

2. On a lightly floured surface, roll out dough to ¼-inch thickness. Cut out palm trees. (See drawing.) Place on lightly greased baking sheet. Brush top with egg white.

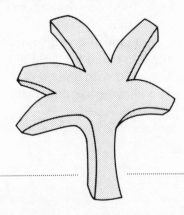

3. Bake in a preheated 350°F oven 10 to 15 minutes, or until golden brown. If cookies have spread while baking, trim into shape. Cool on a wire rack.

4. To make icing: Combine sugar, almond extract, and water. Mix. If desired, reserve ¼ cup of the icing and add green food coloring. Mix. Set aside. Frost trees with remaining icing. Fill writing tip and pastry bag with green icing. Outline ribs and edges of palm leaves.

Fig Turnover

The association of figs with Palm Sunday led to this diminutive turnover—a port-soaked fig in a cream cheese crust. A distinctive treat. *Yields 2½ dozen*

> 1¾ *cups all-purpose flour*
> ½ *teaspoon salt*
> 1 *stick butter*
> 4 *ounces cream cheese*
> 30 *dried figs*
> ¾ *cup port wine*
> *melted butter*
>
> *baking sheet*

1. In a mixing bowl, combine flour, salt, butter, and cream cheese. Mix thoroughly. Chill overnight. Soak figs in port overnight.

2. Roll out dough to ⅛-inch thickness. Cut into 3-inch circles. Drain figs. Dip figs into melted butter. Place 1 fig in the center of each circle and wrap dough around it. Place seam side down on baking sheet.

3. Bake in a preheated 375°F oven 15 to 20 minutes, or until golden brown. Cool on a wire rack.

Fig Pie

In parts of England the eating of fig pie, sometimes called fag pie, was a cherished tradition on Palm Sunday. This pie, topped with whipped cream, is reminiscent of mince pie but not so rich. *Yields 1 pie*

(For pie crust ingredients see page 4.)
2½ cups dry figs
⅓ cup currants
2 tablespoons dark molasses
1½ cups granulated sugar
1 tablespoon grated orange rind
½ teaspoon ground cinnamon
¼ teaspoon ground cloves
¼ teaspoon ground nutmeg
3 egg whites

Topping
1 cup heavy cream
1 tablespoon confectioners' sugar
½ teaspoon vanilla extract

9-inch pie plate

(For pie crust preparation see page 4.)
1. Boil figs until tender in just enough water to cover them. Chop coarsely.
2. In a mixing bowl, combine figs, currants, molasses, sugar, orange rind, and spices. Mix. Set aside.
3. Beat egg whites until stiff peaks stand up. Fold into fig mixture.
4. Pour into baked pie crust. Bake in a preheated 450°F oven 10 minutes. Lower heat to 350°F and bake about 30 minutes more. Cool.
5. When ready to serve pie: In a chilled bowl, beat cream,

sugar, and vanilla extract until stiff peaks stand up. Spread topping over pie.

NOTE: Can be made as an open or double crust pie. (I prefer the latter.)

Fig Pudding

Palm Sunday has long meant fig pudding in England. As noted, figs and fig desserts were associated with the day—because of Jesus' encounter with a fig tree on his entry into Jerusalem. Topped with hard sauce, this pudding never fails to please. *Yields 1 pudding*

> ⅔ cup light brown sugar, firmly packed
> 1¼ cups fresh bread crumbs
> 1 teaspoon ground nutmeg
> 1 teaspoon ground ginger
> 1 cup all-purpose flour
> ¼ teaspoon salt
> 2 eggs
> 1 cup milk
> 2¼ cups dry figs, finely chopped
> ½ cup ground suet

Hard Sauce
> 1 stick butter
> 1⅓ cups confectioners' sugar
> 2–3 tablespoons brandy

> 2-quart pudding mold

1. In a large mixing bowl, combine sugar, bread crumbs, spices, flour, and salt. Mix.

2. Add eggs and milk to flour mixture. Stir in figs and suet. Mix.

3. Pour into greased mold. Snap cover tight on mold. Place in a large kettle. Pour in water ⅔ of the way up the sides of the mold. Cover. Boil, then lower heat. Simmer until a toothpick comes out clean, about 4 hours. Add more boiling water as necessary.

4. Remove mold from kettle. Cool pudding to room temperature. (Pudding may be stored in refrigerator about 2 weeks.)

To make hard sauce:
In a mixing bowl, cream butter and sugar until light and fluffy. Gradually beat in brandy. Place in a serving dish and cover. Store in refrigerator.

To reheat pudding:
Place mold on a rack in a large pot. Pour in boiling water ⅔ of the way up the sides of the mold. Bring to a boil, and simmer 2 hours. Remove mold from the pot. Carefully remove pudding from mold onto serving plate.

To serve pudding:
Top reheated pudding with hard sauce.

Moravian Love Cookies

Holy Saturday, celebrated on the morning (or formerly, the evening) before Easter, marks the ending of Lent. At this time, the devout light new fires, hold religious processions, remove the veils from statues, and make other preparations for Easter according to local tradition. The Moravians brought to the United States the delightful Holy Saturday custom of serving these spicy cookies with coffee before a service at the dawning of Easter Day. *Yields 18 cookies 4 × 2 inches*

> 1 cup honey
> 2 tablespoons granulated sugar
> 1/3 cup finely chopped almonds
> 1/3 cup candied orange peel, finely chopped
> 1/2 teaspoon baking soda
> 1/4 teaspoon ground nutmeg
> 1 teaspoon ground cinnamon
> 1/4 teaspoon ground cloves
> 2 tablespoons sherry
> 1 3/4 cups all-purpose flour
> granulated sugar for sprinkling on top
>
> baking sheet

1. In a mixing bowl, combine honey and sugar. Add almonds and orange peel. Mix. Add baking soda, spices, and sherry. Mix thoroughly.
2. Gradually add flour. (Dough should be stiff enough to roll out.) Chill overnight.
3. Roll out dough to 1/8-inch thickness. Cut into 4 by 2-inch pieces. (Make pieces smaller if you wish.) Sprinkle sugar on top of cookies. Place on lightly greased baking sheet.
4. Bake in a preheated 350°F oven 15 to 20 minutes, until firm. Cool on a wire rack.

NOTE: Store in an airtight container.

7

PURIM

Purim is one of the most jubilant Jewish festivals. The celebration commemorates Esther, Jewish queen of King Ahasuerus of Persia. It falls on the fourteenth day of the Hebrew month of Adar—in February or March.

The Megillah, scroll of Esther, tells how Haman, the Persian king's first minister, talked the king into planning to destroy all the Jews in his kingdom. Esther's cousin Mordecai discovered the plot and called on Esther to change the king's mind. She did so and saved her people.

Israel celebrates Purim as a national holiday. There masqueraders throng the streets in an outpouring of joy at the saving of the Persian Jews. Jewish communities in New York City mark Purim with a number of public parties. New York University has been the scene of a Queen Esther's Block Party, with folk music, clowns, and Middle Eastern delicacies. Jewish communities across the nation sponsor parties, parades, and concerts, along with readings from the Megillah of Esther. Countless private parties carry out the theme of boisterous rejoicing at Esther's triumph.

Much good cooking is associated with Purim. The most renowned Purim dessert is hamantashen—"Haman's pockets." These triangular pastries, filled with poppyseeds or preserves, represent the villain Haman's pocket or three-cornered hat, the symbol of his high position in the Persian government.

Moroccan Cookies for Purim

Moroccan Jews bake these sugar cookies for Purim. The cookies are served on the morning of Purim along with other special treats. *Yields about 2–2½ dozen*

> 3 *sticks butter*
> ¾ *cup granulated sugar*
> 2⅔ *cups all-purpose flour*
> ½ *cup finely ground almonds or walnuts*
> *cinnamon for sprinkling on top*
>
> *baking sheet*

1. In a mixing bowl, cream butter and sugar until light and fluffy. Gradually add flour.

2. Knead dough until smooth. Then knead in nuts until dough feels smooth.

3. Take golf ball-size pieces of dough and roll into smooth balls. Flatten balls slightly on baking sheet. Sprinkle cinnamon on the center of each cookie.

4. Bake in a preheated 350°F oven 35 to 45 minutes. *Cookies should not be allowed to brown.*

NOTE: Store in an airtight container.

Hamantashen—"Haman's Pockets"

(HAH-mun-tash-en)

These pastries, triangular in shape, resemble the pocket or hat (depending on your source) of Haman, the hated prime minister of ancient Persia. They are eaten as a show of defiance against him. Take your pick of poppyseed or prune filling—both are given here. *Yields about 5 dozen*

> 4 cups all-purpose flour
> 1/2 tablespoon baking powder
> 2/3 cup granulated sugar
> 1/4 teaspoon salt
> 4 eggs
> 1/3 cup vegetable oil
> 1 tablespoon grated lemon rind

Poppyseed Filling
2/3 cup ground poppyseeds
1/3 cup granulated sugar
1/3 cup dark raisins
1/3 cup finely chopped dates
1/2 cup honey
1 egg
1/2 teaspoon ground cinnamon
1 tablespoon grated orange rind

Prune Filling
1 pound prunes
4 thin orange slices
2/3 cup chopped walnuts
1/2 cup lemon juice
1 tablespoon grated lemon rind
1/3 cup granulated sugar
1/2 tablespoon ground cinnamon
1/2 teaspoon ground nutmeg

3-inch round cookie cutter

1. In a mixing bowl, combine flour, baking powder, sugar, and salt. Stir in eggs, oil, and lemon rind. Mix thoroughly.

2. On a lightly floured surface, roll out dough to ⅛-inch thickness. Cut into rounds. Make filling (see below). Drop a generous teaspoonful of filling in center of each round. Draw up two sides; then draw up the third across to form a triangle. Pinch edges together, allowing a little of the filling to show.

3. Place on lightly greased baking sheet. Bake in a preheated 350°F oven 20 to 30 minutes, or until golden brown. Cool on a wire rack.

To make fillings:

Poppyseed: In a saucepan, combine filling ingredients. Simmer 10 minutes, stirring constantly. Cool and use.

Prune: In a saucepan, cook prunes and orange slices until tender. Cool sufficiently to permit handling of prunes. Stone and chop fine. Add rest of ingredients. Mix and use.

8

MOTHER ANN'S BIRTHDAY

MARCH 1

Mother Ann Lee's eccentric but inspired career was responsible for launching the Shaker religious sect in the United States—the origin of some of the finest craftwork in the nation's history as well as of some of the best cooking.

Born in 1736, Ann Lee reached adulthood outwardly like innumerable young women of her time in England. At the age of twenty-two she joined an offshoot of the Quakers that emphasized fasting and visionary experiences. The group came to be known as the Shakers because of the way some shook during their devotions. Ann married a blacksmith and had four children, all of whom died in infancy. She came to believe that the "cohabitation" of the sexes was sinful. After being persecuted in Manchester for her religious views, Ann went to America in 1774 with eight followers including her husband. They regarded her as their spiritual mother.

Mother Ann founded a Shaker settlement in what is now Watervliet, New York. Members of the settlement held all property in common and forswore marriage. (Ann and her husband had already parted company.) Although she suffered persecution in America as in England, Mother Ann spread the news of her visions, preaching in New England as well as New York State. In 1784 she died, triumphant in the knowledge that her teachings were fruitful.

Mother Ann's word lived on. Shaker communities arose in Massachusetts, Connecticut, New Hampshire, Maine, and other states. Converts pursued the trades and crafts they had practiced in the outside world. The difference was their work became suffused with the simplicity and purity of Shaker teachings. Shaker innovations in furniture design, agriculture, technology, and other arts and crafts are widely celebrated. Now the Shakers seem destined to die out, the result of their refusal to allow marriage and the propagation of children in their settlements. But their personal and artistic achievements remain as cultural landmarks—superb and simple cooking not being the least.

Mother Ann's Birthday Cake

Mother Ann Lee, leader of the Shakers in the United States, was born on February 29, but her birthday is celebrated by the Shakers on March 1. This white cake was traditionally served at supper after an afternoon meeting that commemorated her life. The cake's delicate flavor is enhanced by the peach jam filling. *Yields 1 cake*

2¾ cups all-purpose flour
⅓ cup cornstarch
1 tablespoon baking powder
½ teaspoon salt
2 sticks butter
1½ cups granulated sugar
¾ cup milk
1 teaspoon vanilla extract
10 egg whites, beaten
peach jam

Frosting
1¼ cups granulated sugar
⅔ cup boiling water
1 egg white
¼ teaspoon cream of tartar
1 teaspoon peach jam

3 8-inch cake pans

1. In a bowl, combine flour, cornstarch, baking powder, and salt. Set aside. In a mixing bowl, cream butter and sugar until light and fluffy.

2. Gradually add flour mixture and milk alternately. Add vanilla. Mix thoroughly.

3. Fold in egg whites. Place batter in three greased and lightly floured cake pans. Bake in a preheated 350°F oven 35 to 40 minutes, or until a cake tester comes out clean. Cool on a wire rack.

4. To make frosting: In a mixing bowl, combine sugar, water, egg white, cream of tartar, and peach jam. Beat rapidly about 7 minutes, until stiff peaks stand up.

5. Stir peach jam mixture. Place cake on a serving plate with peach jam spread between layers of the cake. Frost sides and top.

9

SAINT JOSEPH'S DAY

MARCH 19

Saint Joseph enjoys special popularity in Italy, where his feast day was formerly a national holiday. Italians celebrate his feast in a variety of ways hallowed by tradition. In many towns people parade through the main streets behind his statue. Church members in Sicily prepare and serve a meal for the poor in Joseph's honor. Some Sicilians hold an open house on Saint Joseph's Day and serve a meal at which three children portray the Holy Family. Another Italian tradition is to serve twelve dishes at his feast to symbolize the apostles.

The Virgin Mary's husband, Joseph is a somewhat shadowy figure in the Bible. Little is known of his life after he took the twelve-year-old Jesus to the Passover Feast in Jerusalem. But starting in the 1200's, interest in Joseph grew rapidly.

The Episcopal, Eastern Orthodox, and Roman Catholic churches regard Joseph as a saint. He is honored in the Roman Catholic Church as the patron saint of workers (he was a carpenter by trade) and the protector of the family. His feast day falls on March 19 for the Roman Catholic Church and many Episcopal churches. Eastern Orthodox churches celebrate his feast on the Sunday after Christmas.

Desserts rank high among Saint Joseph's feast delicacies. One of the noteworthy is a kind of cream puff filled with ricotta cheese or flavored custard. This and the other desserts in this chapter add to the festiveness of a holiday rich in medieval overtones.

Saint Joseph's Cream Puffs

These cream puffs are a tremendous favorite at Saint Joseph's Day festivals. Fillings, all of them delectable, vary from one region of Italy to another. This one consists of ricotta cheese flavored with orange and lemon peel and crème de cacao. Note that these puffs are baked; some versions are deep fried. *Yields 12*

Puffs
1 cup water
1 stick butter
1 cup all-purpose flour
¼ teaspoon salt
4 eggs
2 tablespoons granulated sugar
1 teaspoon grated orange peel
1 teaspoon grated lemon peel

Filling
1 pound ricotta cheese
3 teaspoons chocolate bits, finely chopped
¼ cup granulated sugar
½ tablespoon grated orange peel
2 tablespoons crème de cacao
confectioners' sugar for sprinkling on top

baking sheet

Puffs
1. In a saucepan, bring water and butter to a boil. Lower heat. Add flour and salt, stirring well. Keep stirring until the mixture leaves the sides of the pan.

2. Remove from heat. Add eggs 1 at a time, beating after each addition. Add sugar and fruit peels.

3. Place dough on greased baking sheet 1 tablespoon at a time, about 2 inches apart. Bake in a preheated 375°F oven 30 minutes, or until golden brown. Cool on a wire rack.

Filling
Mix filling ingredients. Fill cooled puffs. Sprinkle with confectioners' sugar.

NOTE: Refrigerate. Eat within a day of filling puffs.

Crema de San José—Saint Joseph's Custard

(CRAY-ma day sahn ho-ZAY)

This creamy custard honors Saint Joseph in Spain. It may be topped with whipped cream and served with ladyfingers. *Yields 4–6 servings*

> 3 tablespoons cornstarch
> ½ cup cold milk
> 6 egg yolks
> ⅔ cup granulated sugar
> ¼ teaspoon salt
> 1 cinnamon stick, broken into 4 pieces
> 1 tablespoon grated lemon peel
> 1½ cups milk, scalded
> ⅓ cup granulated sugar, for sprinkling on top
> sweetened whipped cream (optional)
>
> 9-inch pie plate

1. Dissolve cornstarch in milk. In a saucepan, combine egg yolks, sugar, salt, and cornstarch mixture. Add cinnamon stick and lemon peel. Slowly add scalded milk.
2. Cook over medium heat 6 to 8 minutes, stirring constantly. (Do not allow to boil—eggs will curdle.) Remove from heat.
3. Strain. Let cool to room temperature. To prevent film from

forming on the surface, stir occasionally. After pudding has cooled, cover and refrigerate 4 to 6 hours.

4. Shortly before serving, sprinkle sugar on surface. To caramelize and harden sugar, place pudding under a preheated broiler 5 minutes. (Do not leave any longer—custard will become soupy.) Wait a few minutes before serving. Top with whipped cream if desired.

Saint Joseph's Fig Cookies

A fig-fruit filling in tender pastry makes these cookies an unforgettable treat at Saint Joseph's Day celebrations. *Yields about 3 dozen*

> ½ cup dried figs
> ¼ cup pitted chopped dates
> ¼ cup golden raisins
> ¼ cup candied cherries, coarsely chopped
> ¼ cup blanched almonds, coarsely chopped
> ½ teaspoon ground cinnamon
> ¼ teaspoon ground cloves
> 3 tablespoons hot water
> 2 tablespoons honey

Dough
2¾ cups all-purpose flour
½ cup granulated sugar
½ tablespoon baking powder
¼ teaspoon salt
1 stick butter
¾ cup milk
1 teaspoon vanilla extract

Lemon Glaze
3 cups confectioners' sugar
¼ cup water
½ tablespoon lemon juice

baking sheet

1. To make filling: In a food processor or food grinder, combine figs, dates, raisins, cherries, and almonds. Mince finely. Place in a bowl. Add cinnamon, cloves, hot water, and honey. Mix thoroughly and set aside.

2. To make dough: In a mixing bowl, combine flour, sugar, baking powder, and salt. Cut in butter. Add milk and vanilla. Mix.

3. On a lightly floured surface, knead dough about 5 minutes, or until smooth. Roll out dough to ⅛-inch thickness. Cut into 3-inch squares. Place 1 tablespoon of filling in the center of each square. Fold opposite corners toward each other.

4. Place on lightly greased baking sheet. Bake in a preheated 350°F oven 15 to 20 minutes, or until golden brown. Cool on a wire rack.

5. To make glaze: In a mixing bowl, combine sugar, water, and lemon juice. Mix thoroughly. Drizzle on cooled cookies.

Saint Joseph's Wood Shavings

These deep-fried pastries from Spain charmingly imitate the shavings that curled from Joseph's plane as he followed his trade. *Yields 3 dozen*

6 tablespoons butter
⅓ cup lard
½ cup granulated sugar
2 eggs
3 tablespoons port wine
1 teaspoon grated lemon rind
1 teaspoon grated orange rind
½ teaspoon ground cinnamon
2⅔ cups all-purpose flour
vegetable oil for frying
confectioners' sugar for sprinkling on top

deep fryer or other deep pan for frying;
36 craft sticks or Popsicle sticks

1. In a mixing bowl, combine butter, lard, and sugar. Beat until light and fluffy. Add eggs, wine, fruit rinds, and cinnamon. Gradually add flour. Mix thoroughly.

2. Roll out pieces of dough to form ropes about as thick as a pencil and 6 inches long. Wrap dough the length of craft sticks.

3. Heat oil to 375°F. Fry a few at a time until golden brown —less than a minute. Turn over once.

4. Remove and drain on paper towels. *Do not remove from sticks.* Remove sticks when completely cooled. Sprinkle with confectioners' sugar.

NOTE: Store in an airtight container.

10

PASSOVER

For over three thousand years, the Jews have celebrated Passover. This spring festival, among the most revered in the Jewish calendar, commemorates the deliverance of the Hebrews from Egyptian bondage. Passover starts on the fourteenth day in the Hebrew month of Nisan, March or April, and continues eight days.

The events Passover reflects have an epic quality. Jews celebrating the holiday remember the years of slavery their ancestors endured under Egypt's Pharaoh, the ten plagues God visited on the Egyptians for not releasing the Jews, forty years wandering in the desert, and arrival in the Promised land. The Jews were *passed over*, spared, when the Angel of Death slew the firstborn children of the Egyptians, hence the holiday's name.

A highlight of Passover is the Seder, a service and ceremonial dinner held on the first evening of Passover. (The Seder is often repeated on the second night except in Israel.) This service is outlined in the Haggadah, a special Passover prayer book given to each participant. Foods eaten at the Seder have symbolic importance. The matzoh, unleavened bread, reminds celebrants that their ancestors had to leave Egypt so hurriedly there was no time to let their bread rise. A bitter herb, often horseradish, stands for the bitterness of slavery. A green such as parsley signifies that Passover is a spring festival. A roasted lamb bone is a reminder of the lamb whose blood was smeared on Israelite doorposts to ward off the Angel of Death. A roasted egg harks back to the offering in Jerusalem's ancient temple. Haroset, a paste of fruit and nuts flavored with cinnamon, signifies the mortar that the Jewish slaves had to use in laying bricks during their Egyptian bondage. Salt water symbolizes the tears of servitude.

Despite the somber events it embodies, the Seder is a joyous feast of salvation. Concluding it are desserts in this happy spirit. Haroset is a favorite dessert, but recipes vary from one part of the world to another. Jews with a European background often use chopped apples; Jews with an Oriental background may include dates in the ingredients. But the Passover offers a wide range of desserts originating in Jewish communities all over the world.

Haroset—Passover Fruit Paste

(ha-ROHS-et)

The sweetness of haroset counteracts the Seder's bitter herbs. It is eaten by itself or spread on matzoh. *Yields about 3 cups*

> 2 *cups dark raisins*
> 1 *cup chopped pitted dates*
> *granulated sugar to taste*
> 1/2 *cup sweet red Passover wine*
> 1/2 *cup walnuts for sprinkling on top*
>
> *glass bowl*

1. In a bowl, place raisins and dates. Add enough water to cover. Set aside 1 hour. Add sugar and wine. Purée mixture in a blender 1/4 cup at a time. (Or mix in a food processor 1/3 at a time.)
2. Spoon into a saucepan. Simmer over a low heat about 20 minutes, or until liquid is absorbed.
3. Spoon into glass bowl. Top with chopped nuts.

Passover Nut Cookies

These crunchy cookies filled with ground filberts are a wholesome Passover treat that never palls. *Yields 4½ dozen*

> 6 eggs
> ¾ cup granulated sugar
> ½ tablespoon grated lemon rind
> 3 tablespoons vegetable oil
> 1¼ cups coarsely ground filberts
> 1¼ cups matzoh cake meal
> 2 tablespoons potato starch
> ¼ teaspoon salt
> granulated sugar for sprinkling on top
>
> baking sheet

1. In a mixing bowl, combine eggs, sugar, and lemon rind. Beat until light and fluffy. Add remaining ingredients. Mix thoroughly.
2. Drop by the spoonful on ungreased baking sheet. Sprinkle sugar lightly over cookies. Bake in a preheated 400°F oven 10 to 15 minutes, or until golden brown. Cool on a wire rack.

Hadgi Badam—Passover Macaroons

Jews in Baghdad, Iraq, traditionally made this delightful almond macaroon for their Passover celebration. *Yields about 5 dozen*

> 3 *cups blanched almonds, finely ground*
> 1 *cup confectioners' sugar*
> ½ *teaspoon ground cardamom*
> 2 *egg whites*
> 1 *tablespoon rosewater*
>
> *baking sheet*

1. In a mixing bowl, combine almonds, sugar, cardamom, and egg whites. Mix thoroughly and knead about 5 minutes.

2. Divide paste into pieces about the size of a walnut. Dampen the palms of your hands with rosewater and roll paste into smooth balls. Dampen your hands again as necessary.

3. Place balls on ungreased baking sheet. Bake in a preheated 375°F oven 10 to 12 minutes, or until golden brown. Cool in baking sheet 3 minutes; then cool on a wire rack.

Passover Nut Cake

One of the most splendid Passover desserts is this nut cake, at once rich and subtle. *Yields 1 cake*

> 9 eggs, separated
> 2 cups granulated sugar
> 1/2 teaspoon ground cinnamon
> 1/4 teaspoon ground cloves
> 1 cup potato starch
> 1 teaspoon lemon juice
> 2 cups walnuts, coarsely ground
> raspberry preserves
> confectioners' sugar for sprinkling on top
>
> 2 8-inch round cake pans

1. In a mixing bowl, beat egg yolks 10 minutes at high speed. Gradually add sugar, cinnamon, cloves, and potato starch. Mix. Add lemon juice and nuts.

2. In a separate mixing bowl, beat egg whites until stiff peaks stand up. Gently fold egg whites into batter.

3. Pour batter into well-greased pans. Bake in a preheated 350°F oven 45 to 55 minutes, or until a cake tester comes out clean. Invert pan on a wire rack. When cake is cool, remove from pan.

4. Place 1 layer on a cake plate. Top with raspberry preserves. Place other layer on top. Sprinkle with confectioners' sugar.

11

EASTER

Easter is Christianity's chief festival, a rejoicing in Christ's Resurrection after His Crucifixion. The impact of Easter is all the more poignant because it follows Christ's Passion—His sufferings between the night of His Last Supper and His death on the cross. Two days passed before His tomb was found, open and mysteriously empty. His disciples soon began to encounter him abroad, risen from the dead.

Easter is a movable feast that falls between March 22 and April 25. As a spring holiday, it incorporates many religious traditions that preceded Christianity. In spring, religions around the world have long celebrated the revival of life that had been apparently dead. Many Easter symbols derive from those earlier used throughout the world to symbolize creation and rebirth. According to the legends of ancient Egypt, India, and Persia, for example, the earth originated from a cosmic egg.

Easter is especially influenced by the Jewish Passover. The Last Supper was a Seder, the Passover ceremonial dinner with symbolic reminders not only of the Hebrew exodus from Egypt but of spiritual rebirth. Pasch, from the Hebrew *pesah,* now refers either to Passover or Easter.

Several festivals follow upon Easter. Whitsunday, or Pentecost, falls on the seventh Sunday after Easter and celebrates the descent of the Holy Spirit on the Apostles. Corpus Christi falls on the Thursday after the eighth Sunday after Easter and celebrates the Eucharist, or sacrament of the Lord's Supper.

As the major Christian holiday, Easter is celebrated in ways that are drenched in pageantry, symbolism, and tradition. Food plays an important part in many Easter observances. Hard-boiled eggs, often elaborately decorated, are an important part of Easter festivities around the world. Lamb is a popular Easter main course representing Jesus and linking His death to the lamb sacrificed on the first Passover. Easter breads, such as babka and kulich from Eastern Europe, are often blessed by a priest before being served with Easter dinner.

Here is a broad selection of Easter, and a few post-Easter, desserts from around the world—cookies, cakes, puddings, and candy—all embodying the joyful heritage of Easter.

Simnel Cake

Older even than Christianity, this rich cake has been associated for centuries with the Easter season. In Britain, simnel cakes were formerly baked for Mothering Sunday, when children honored their parents with gifts of flowers and the cake. But now simnel cakes are usually made for Easter itself. *Yields 1 cake*

Cake Batter
2 *sticks butter*
1 *cup granulated sugar*
4 *eggs*
2 *cups all-purpose flour*
²/₃ *cup currants*
¹/₃ *cup candied orange peel, finely chopped*
¹/₃ *cup candied lemon peel, finely chopped*
1 *tablespoon grated lemon rind*
¹/₄ *teaspoon salt*
¹/₄ *teaspoon baking soda*
almond paste (see page 4)

Butter Cream Frosting
1½ sticks butter
4 cups sifted confectioners' sugar
1 egg yolk
1 teaspoon almond extract
3 tablespoons (or more if desired) water

8-inch springform pan

Cake
1. Grease pan. Line with wax paper and grease paper.
2. In a mixing bowl, cream butter and sugar until light and fluffy. Add eggs 1 at a time, beating after each addition.
3. In a small bowl, reserve ¼ cup of the flour. Add currants, candied fruit peels, and lemon rind. Mix.
4. Add remaining flour and other dry ingredients to the batter. Fold fruit into batter.
5. Pour ½ of batter into pan. Roll almond paste to fit into 8-inch pan. Place on top of batter. Add remaining batter. (See note.)
6. Bake in a preheated 300°F oven 2 hours, or until a cake tester comes out clean. Cool cake 15 minutes. Then cool on a wire rack.

Butter Cream Frosting
In a mixing bowl, cream butter and sugar until light and fluffy. Mix in egg yolk and almond extract. Add water for the consistency you desire. Frost sides and top of cake.

NOTES: If you wish, buy almond paste, available in the gourmet section of grocery stores.

For three-layer cake: Use ⅓ of batter for each layer. Divide almond paste in half for use between layers.

Sedgemoor Easter Cookies

These delightful Easter cookies ("cakes" in British usage) help welcome Easter in rural Britain. The currants and brandy in the cookies give them a mellow flavor. Serve them once and your family and friends will insist that you make them an Easter tradition of your own. *Yields about 3 dozen*

> 1 1/2 cups flour
> 1 stick butter
> 2/3 cup granulated sugar
> 1/4 cup currants
> 1 teaspoon ground cinnamon
> 1/2 teaspoon ground allspice
> 1/2 teaspoon ground cloves
> 1 egg
> 3 tablespoons brandy
>
> *2-inch round cookie cutter; baking sheet*

1. In a mixing bowl, combine flour, butter, sugar, currants, and spices. Mix.
2. Add egg and brandy. Mix thoroughly. Refrigerate about 1 hour.
3. On a lightly floured surface, roll out dough to 1/2-inch thickness. Cut with round cookie cutter. Place on a baking sheet. Bake in a preheated 350°F oven 12 to 15 minutes, or until firm to the touch. Cool on a wire rack.

NOTE: These cookies freeze well.

English Easter Fruit Cookies

These fruit cookies come from Gloucestershire. Their delicate but distinctive flavor explains why they have been passed down from generation to generation. *Yields 3½ dozen*

> ½ cup confectioners' sugar
> 1 stick butter
> 3 tablespoons lard
> 2 eggs
> 1 tablespoon grated lemon rind
> 1½ cups all-purpose flour
> ¼ cup currants
> ¼ cup mixed candied fruit peel, finely chopped
>
> *2-inch round cookie cutter; baking sheet*

1. In a mixing bowl, cream sugar, butter, and lard until light and fluffy. Add eggs, lemon rind, and 1¼ cups of the flour. Mix.
2. In a small bowl, mix currants, fruit, and remaining flour together. Stir into batter. Chill overnight.
3. On a lightly floured surface, roll out dough to ¼-inch thickness. Using round cookie cutter, cut out cookies.
4. Place on lightly greased baking sheet. Bake in a preheated 350°F oven 8 to 10 minutes, or until golden brown. Cool on a wire rack.

NOTE: Store in an airtight container.

Italian Easter Turnovers

These miniature turnovers are a must at Eastertime in parts of southern Italy. Filled with jam, walnuts, and brandy, they are an irresistible holiday snack. *Yields about 30*

Pastry Dough
1¾ cups all-purpose flour
½ teaspoon salt
1 stick butter
¼ cup granulated sugar
4–5 tablespoons ice water

Filling
½ cup grape jam or jelly
⅓ cup granulated sugar
½ teaspoon ground cinnamon
⅓ cup finely ground walnuts
¼ cup cocoa
1 tablespoon brandy

water
egg yolk for glaze

3-inch round cookie cutter; baking sheet

1. For pastry dough: In a mixing bowl, combine flour, salt, butter, and sugar. Gradually add cold water 1 tablespoon at a time. Stop when dough can be gathered into a ball. Make ball and stop handling. Wrap in foil or plastic wrap. Set aside.
2. To make filling: In a small mixing bowl, combine grape jam, sugar, cinnamon, walnuts, cocoa, and brandy. Set aside.
3. Roll out pastry dough to about ⅛-inch thickness. Using cookie cutter, cut dough into rounds. Put a spoonful of filling into the center of each round. Moisten edge of each round and fold in half. With a fork, press edge together. With a knife point, prick each top. Brush with egg yolk.

4. Place on ungreased baking sheet. Bake in a preheated 375°F oven 10 to 15 minutes, or until golden brown.

NOTES: If at the end of step 2, jelly is not firm, combine 1 table-spoon of potato starch with 1 teaspoon of water. Heat jelly mix-ture together with potato starch. Cool before using.

Serve hot or cold. The turnovers freeze well.

Italian Easter Pie

A widespread favorite in Italy on Easter, this pie (or some would say cake) is a joyous blend of ricotta cheese, candied fruit, cinna-mon, and lemon peel. *Yields 1 pie*

Crust *(Pasta Frolla)*
2 cups all-purpose flour
½ teaspoon salt
1 teaspoon baking powder
1 teaspoon grated lemon rind
1 stick butter
½ cup granulated sugar
2 eggs

Filling
½ cup quick-cooking tapioca
¼ teaspoon salt
1 tablespoon granulated sugar
½ tablespoon ground cinnamon
2 cups milk
1 pound ricotta cheese
¾ cup granulated sugar
4 eggs, separated
½ teaspoon salt

½ *tablespoon grated lemon rind*
2 *tablespoons lemon juice*
¾ *cup mixed candied fruit peel, finely chopped*
confectioners' sugar for sprinkling on top (optional)

9-inch springform pan

1. In a bowl, combine flour, salt, baking powder, and lemon rind. In a mixing bowl, cream butter and sugar together until light and fluffy.

2. Add eggs 1 at a time, beating after each addition. Gradually add flour mixture. Mix thoroughly. Cover and chill.

3. To make filling: In a saucepan, combine tapioca, salt, 1 tablespoon sugar, and cinnamon. Gradually add milk. Boil 5 minutes, stirring constantly. Cool. Set aside.

4. In a mixing bowl, beat ricotta until smooth. Add sugar and egg yolks 1 at a time, beating after each addition. Add salt, lemon rind, lemon juice, and candied fruit peel.

5. In mixing bowl, beat egg whites until stiff peaks stand up. Fold egg whites into ricotta mixture. Fold in tapioca mixture. Set aside.

6. Grease pan. Roll out ⅔ of dough to cover bottom of pan and about 1½ inches up the sides. Place dough in pan. Pour in ricotta mixture.

7. Cut remaining crust into 1-inch strips. Crisscross strips over ricotta mixture. Trim around edges. Bake in a preheated 350°F oven 50 to 60 minutes, or until crust is golden brown and cooked through. Let cool in pan. When cool, serve. Sprinkle with confectioners' sugar if desired.

Oster Mandel Bäckerei—Easter Almond Cookies

(OH-ster MAHN-del BEK-er-eye)

The Viennese serve these delicate almond cookies as one of the special treats for their celebration of Easter. *Yields about 2 dozen*

> 2 *cups blanched almonds, finely ground*
> 1/2 *cup granulated sugar*
> 1 *egg*
> 1 *teaspoon cognac*
>
> *baking sheet*

1. In a mixing bowl, combine almonds and sugar. Mix. Add egg and cognac. Mix thoroughly.
2. Drop 1 teaspoon at a time on greased baking sheet. Bake in a preheated 350°F oven 10 to 15 minutes, or until golden brown.
3. Leave on baking sheet 5 minutes. Then cool on a wire rack.

Osterbäckerei—Viennese Easter Cookies

(OH-ster-BEK-er-EYE)

These lemon-almond cookies, an Easter treat in Vienna, will enhance your Easter too. *Yields 2½ dozen*

1 *stick butter*
⅓ *cup granulated sugar*
½ *tablespoon grated lemon peel*
2 *eggs*
1 *hard-boiled egg yolk, mashed*
½ *tablespoon lemon juice*
1¾ *cups all-purpose flour*
⅓ *cup blanched almonds, finely ground*
1 *egg for glaze*
2 *tablespoons blanched almonds, coarsely chopped*

Easter cookie cutters; baking sheet

1. In a mixing bowl, cream butter and sugar until light and fluffy. Add lemon peel, eggs, egg yolk, and lemon juice. Mix thoroughly.

2. Gradually add flour and finely ground almonds. Mix thoroughly. Refrigerate at least 2 hours.

3. On a lightly floured surface, roll out dough to ⅛-inch thickness. Cut with Easter cookie cutters. Place on greased baking sheet.

4. Beat egg lightly; brush on top of cookies. Sprinkle with chopped almonds. Bake in a preheated 350°F oven 15 to 18 minutes, or until lightly browned. Cool on a wire rack.

NOTE: Store in an airtight container.

Osterfladen—Swiss Easter Pie

(OH-ster-FLAH-den)

German-speaking people of Switzerland traditionally enjoy this creamy pie on Easter. Almonds and raisins, underscored by kirsch, make this dessert uniquely good. *Yields 1 pie*

> *9-inch pie crust, unbaked*
> *¾ cup blanched almonds, finely ground*
> *¾ cup granulated sugar*
> *1¼ cups light cream*
> *⅔ cup milk*
> *2 tablespoons cornstarch*
> *3 eggs, separated*
> *⅔ cup golden raisins*
> *1 tablespoon kirsch*
>
> *pie plate*

1. Make pie crust according to the instructions on page 4.
2. In a mixing bowl, beat almonds, sugar, and cream until smooth. Beat milk and cornstarch together. Add to cream mixture. Add egg yolks 1 at a time, beating after each addition. Add raisins and kirsch. Stir.
3. Beat egg whites until stiff peaks stand up. Gently fold into cream mixture. Bake in a preheated 325°F oven 1 hour and 20 minutes, or until brown. Cool before serving.

Paskha—Russian Cheesecake

(PAHS-khah)

A highlight of the Russian Orthodox Easter is paskha, a rich cheesecake filled with candied fruit and nuts. This delicacy was often taken to Easter services at church for the priest's blessing. The tradition is to make paskha in a special mold with XB on it, standing for "Christ is risen." You can make this dessert just as easily, however, in a clay flowerpot. *Yields cake serving 12*

To prepare Flowerpot:

Use a new clay flowerpot 7 inches tall by 7 inches in diameter across the top, with a hole in the bottom. Wash thoroughly and dry. Bake in a preheated 300°F oven 1 hour, or until thoroughly dry. Cool before using.

To line mold, dampen cheesecloth. Cut a double thickness of the cloth in pieces long enough to drape over inside of mold, with a 2-inch flap.

> 3 pounds farmer cheese
> 2 sticks butter, softened
> ¾ cup heavy cream
> 4 egg yolks
> ¾ cup granulated sugar
> ½ cup chopped candied fruit peel
> 1 teaspoon vanilla extract
> 1 teaspoon grated lemon peel
> 1 cup blanched almonds, finely chopped
> candied fruit peel for garnish
>
> flowerpot; pie plate; cheesecloth

1. Using a wooden spoon, press cheese into a strainer over a bowl (this removes lumps). In a mixing bowl, combine cheese and butter. Mix thoroughly. Set aside.

2. In a large saucepan, heat cream until almost boiling. Cool

slightly. In a separate mixing bowl, beat egg yolks and sugar. Slowly add cream to egg mixture. Stir thoroughly.

3. Return mixture to saucepan. Stir over low heat until mixture thickens to custardlike consistency.

4. Remove from heat. Add cheese mixture, fruit, vanilla, and lemon peel. Mix thoroughly. Cool completely. Fold in nuts.

5. Place lined mold in pie plate or shallow soup plate. Pour mixture in the mold. Cover with flaps of the cheesecloth.

6. Place a heavy weight, such as several cans of food in a pan, on the cheesecloth to press down the mixture. Whey, the watery part of the cheese, will drain out from the mold bottom.

7. Refrigerate at least 24 hours, until firm.

8. Loosen cheesecloth from top. Place serving plate upside down on the pot. Then turn plate and pot over together. Lift off pot. Remove cheesecloth gently.

9. Garnish with candied fruit peel, making traditional letters XB, if desired. To serve: Slice horizontally or cut in small wedges.

NOTES: May be made at least 3 days in advance. May be refrigerated up to 2 weeks.

Wrap pot in plastic for use year after year.

Szerelmes Levél—Hungarian Love Letters, and Austrian Valentine Cookies

Shrove Tuesday Knots and Brandy Snaps

Crema de San José—Saint Joseph's Cream Puffs, and
Saint Joseph's Wood Shavings

Mazurki Bakaliowe—Polish Fruit Cookies, and Babovka

Rosh Hashanah Carrot Cake, and Teiglach—Honey Balls

Pepparkakshus—Swedish Gingerbread House

Springerle Cookies, Bûche de Noël—Yule Log, and
Basler Brunsli—Swiss Christmas Cookies

Schwarzwälder Kirschtorte—Black Forest Cherry Cake

Babka

(BOB-kah)

Babka is the Polish word for "grandmother," and its fluted sides recall a woman's skirt. A delicious Easter cake, delicately flavored with orange and lemon. *Yields 1 cake*

2½ cups all-purpose flour
1 tablespoon baking powder
1 tablespoon grated lemon peel
1 tablespoon cornstarch
½ teaspoon salt
2 sticks butter
1¾ cups granulated sugar
6 eggs
1 teaspoon vanilla extract
¼ cup orange juice
1 tablespoon lemon juice
½ cup golden raisins
2 tablespoons finely ground bread crumbs, for
    dusting pan

Glaze
⅓ cup warm orange juice
1 cup confectioners' sugar

10-inch Bundt pan

1. In a bowl, combine flour, baking powder, lemon peel, cornstarch, and salt. Set aside. In a mixing bowl, cream butter and sugar until light and fluffy. Add eggs 1 at a time, beating after each addition.

2. Gradually add flour mixture, vanilla, ¼ cup of orange juice, and lemon juice. Mix thoroughly. Stir in raisins.

3. Lightly grease pan and dust with bread crumbs. Pour in batter. Bake in a preheated 325°F oven 50 to 60 minutes, or until

a cake tester comes out clean. Cool in pan 10 minutes. Place on a wire rack.

4. To make glaze: Combine orange juice and sugar. Using a fork, poke holes in the top of the cake.

5. Spoon glaze over warm cake. Cool on a wire rack.

Mazurek Wielkanocny—Polish Easter Cookies

(ma-ZOO-rek weel-ka-NOH-k'nee)

On Easter, Poles look forward to these delicate cookies flecked with sliced almonds. A perennial treat. *Yields 6 dozen*

> 2 *sticks butter*
> 1½ *cups confectioners' sugar*
> 4 *hard-boiled egg yolks*
> 2¼ *cups all-purpose flour*
> 1 *teaspoon vanilla extract*
> 1 *egg beaten with 1 tablespoon water for glaze*
> *thinly sliced almonds for sprinkling on top*
>
> *10 × 15-inch baking sheet*

1. In a mixing bowl, cream butter and sugar until light and fluffy. With a wooden spoon, push egg yolks through a fine sieve into butter mixture. Gradually add flour and vanilla. Mix thoroughly.

2. Shape into a ball. Place in a plastic bag and put in freezer 10 minutes. Roll out to fit on greased baking sheet.

3. Brush with egg glaze. Sprinkle almonds on top. Pat almonds down. Bake in a preheated 375°F oven 20 to 25 minutes, or until golden brown. Remove from oven; cool slightly. Cut into 1 by 2-inch rectangles. Cool on a wire rack.

NOTE: Store in an airtight container.

Polish Easter Cheesecake

One of the treats of Polish Easter feasts, this cheesecake is smoothly rich, with a mellow flavor. Cut into bars for serving. *Yields 4½ dozen 1 × 2-inch rectangles*

> 1½ cups all-purpose flour
> ½ tablespoon baking powder
> ¼ teaspoon salt
> ½ stick butter
> 1 egg
> 4 tablespoons sour cream
> ½ cup confectioners' sugar
> ⅔ cup strawberry jam

Filling
> 5 eggs
> 2 cups confectioners' sugar
> 1 teaspoon vanilla extract
> 1 pound ricotta cheese
> 1 stick butter
> ½ teaspoon ground nutmeg
> ¼ teaspoon salt
> ½ tablespoon grated lemon rind
> ¼ cup candied orange peel, finely chopped
> ¼ cup golden raisins

> 9 × 13-inch pan

1. In a mixing bowl, combine flour, baking powder, and salt. Using a pastry blender, cut in butter.

2. In a small bowl, combine egg and sour cream. Pour into flour mixture. Add sugar. Mix. Put in greased pan. Spread dough about 1 inch up sides. Spread jam on top of dough. Set aside.

3. To make filling: In a mixing bowl, beat eggs with sugar. Add vanilla, ricotta, butter, nutmeg, salt, and lemon rind. Mix thoroughly. Stir in orange peel and raisins.

4. Pour filling onto dough. Bake in a preheated 325°F oven 50 to 60 minutes, or until a knife comes out clean. Cool thoroughly before cutting.

Mazurki Bakaliowe—Polish Fruit Cookies

(mah-ZOOR-ki bah-kahl-lee-OV-eh)

For an Easter delight, try this rich fruit-and-nut cookie, a tradition from Poland that will please everyone. *Yields 6 dozen*

> 1 *stick butter*
> 3/4 *cup granulated sugar*
> 2 1/4 *cups all-purpose flour*
> 1/2 *teaspoon salt*
> 1 *egg*
> 1/3 *cup light cream*

> **Topping**
> 1/2 *cup coarsely chopped almonds*
> 3/4 *cup chopped dates*
> 3/4 *cup chopped figs*
> 1/2 *cup dark raisins*
> 1/2 *cup granulated sugar*
> 1 *egg*
> 1/3 *cup lemon juice*
> 1/3 *cup orange juice*
> 1/2 *cup chopped candied cherries*
> 1/2 *cup chopped candied orange peel*

> *10 × 15-inch baking sheet*

1. To make dough: In a mixing bowl, cream butter and sugar together until light and fluffy. Add remaining ingredients. Pat

down in baking sheet and smooth. Bake in a preheated 350°F oven 20 minutes, or until golden brown.

2. While baking, make topping: In a mixing bowl, combine almonds, dates, figs, raisins, sugar, egg, lemon juice, and orange juice. Mix.

3. After dough is baked, spread topping. Bake 15 to 20 minutes more. Cool slightly. Scatter cherries and orange peel on top. While warm, cut into 1 by 2-inch rectangles.

NOTE: Store in an airtight container.

Babovka with Whipped Cream

(BAH-boov-kah)

This superb cake has a whipped cream filling and chocolate icing. It is a Czechoslovakian favorite at Easter. *Yields 1 cake*

> 2 *cups confectioners' sugar*
> 10 *eggs, separated*
> 1 *teaspoon vanilla extract*
> ½ *tablespoon lemon rind*
> ¼ *cup lemon juice*
> 2½ *cups all-purpose flour*
> ½ *tablespoon baking powder*
> 1 *cup whipping cream (sweetened slightly)*
>
> **Icing**
> 2 *ounces unsweetened chocolate*
> 2 *tablespoons butter*
> ½ *cup milk*
> 3 *cups confectioners' sugar*
> 1 *teaspoon vanilla extract*
>
> *12-cup Bundt pan*

(Make cake 1 day before serving.)

1. In a mixing bowl, combine sugar, egg yolks, vanilla, lemon rind, and lemon juice. Gradually add flour and baking powder.

2. Beat egg whites until stiff peaks stand up. Fold into batter. Pour batter into greased and floured Bundt pan. Bake in a preheated 350°F oven 50 to 60 minutes, or until a cake tester comes out clean.

3. *Next day:* Cut ½ inch off flat side of cake. Scoop out inner part of cake, making sure sides stay intact.

4. Beat whipping cream and fill cake. Replace ½ inch of flat side of cake. Place a serving plate upside down on top of cake and invert.

5. To make icing: In a double boiler, combine chocolate, butter, and milk. When chocolate and butter are melted, remove from heat. Cool to lukewarm. Gradually stir in sugar and vanilla. Ice the cake. Keep in refrigerator before serving.

Beranek—Czechoslovakian Lamb Cake

(BEH-rah-neck)

This decorative cake occupies the place of honor on Czech tables during the Easter dinner. The white-frosted Easter lamb has raisin eyes, a candied-cherry mouth, and often a blue satin ribbon with a bell around the neck. (You may cover frosting with coconut if you wish.) This is a plain cake but richly delicious with great eye appeal. Similar cakes are traditionally served in Poland and Italy. *Yields 1 cake*

> 2 cups all-purpose flour
> ½ teaspoon salt
> ½ tablespoon baking powder
> 1 stick butter
> 1 cup granulated sugar
> 3 eggs
> ½ teaspoon almond extract

Frosting
1 *cup granulated sugar*
1 *egg white*
1 *tablespoon light corn syrup*
¼ *teaspoon salt*
3 *tablespoons water*
1 *teaspoon almond extract*
grated coconut (optional)
2 *raisins (for eyes)*
1 *piece candied cherry (for mouth)*

lamb cake mold (available in many department stores and cake specialty shops); baking sheet

1. Grease inside of mold well. Flour lightly.
2. In a small bowl, combine flour, salt, and baking powder. Set aside.
3. In a mixing bowl, cream butter and sugar together until light and fluffy. Add eggs 1 at a time, beating after each addition.
4. Add almond extract. Add flour mixture, mixing thoroughly.
5. In back half of mold, fill ears with batter. Fill face half of mold with batter. Place back half of mold on top of face half and snap together.
6. Place mold face side up on baking sheet. Bake in a preheated 350°F oven 50 to 60 minutes.
7. Place on a wire rack and cool in mold 5 minutes. Lift off back side of mold and allow face side of mold to cool 5 minutes more. Then remove the rest of the cake. Cool on wire rack.
8. To make frosting: In top of a double boiler, combine sugar, egg white, corn syrup, salt, and water. Place over boiling water and beat rapidly about 7 minutes, until stiff peaks stand up.
9. Remove from heat. Add almond extract and beat 1 minute.
10. Place cake on a serving plate. Frost. If desired, add coconut. Insert raisins for eyes and cherry for mouth.

Greek Honey Pie

This cheesecake in a crust is traditional for Easter and Christmas in the Cyclades, the Greek isles off the southeast coast. Honey here makes a luscious blend with a cream cheese base. *Yields 1 pie*

1¾ cups all-purpose flour
½ tablespoon baking powder
¼ teaspoon salt
1 tablespoon granulated sugar
1 stick butter
3–5 tablespoons ice water

Filling

3 8-ounce packages cream cheese
½ cup granulated sugar
1 teaspoon ground cinnamon
¾ cup honey
5 eggs
ground cinnamon for sprinkling on top

10-inch pie plate

1. In a mixing bowl, combine flour, baking powder, salt, and sugar. With a pastry blender, cut in butter until mixture looks like cornmeal.

2. Gradually add cold water 1 tablespoon at a time. Toss with a fork after each addition. Stop when dough can be gathered into a ball. Make ball and stop handling. Wrap in foil or plastic wrap. Refrigerate at least 30 minutes. Roll out and put in a pie plate.

3. To make filling: In a mixing bowl, beat cream cheese, sugar, and cinnamon. Add honey and eggs 1 at a time, beating after each addition.

4. Pour into prepared pie plate. Bake in a preheated 350°F oven 1 hour. Five minutes before removing from oven, sprinkle cinnamon on top of pie. Cool before serving.

Koulourákia—Greek Easter Cookies

(kou-lou-RAH-ki-a)

These sesame seed–topped cookies are a favorite in Greece at Eastertime. Shape them in the whimsical Greek style—as figure eights, esses, circles, triangles, or little braids. *Yields 5 dozen*

> *3¼ cups all-purpose flour*
> *1 teaspoon baking powder*
> *½ teaspoon ground cinnamon*
> *½ teaspoon ground allspice*
> *1 stick butter*
> *1 cup granulated sugar*
> *4 eggs*
> *1 teaspoon vanilla extract*
> *2 teaspoons anise extract or 4 tablespoons anisette liqueur*
> *1 egg yolk beaten with 1 tablespoon water for glaze sesame seeds for sprinkling on top*
>
> *baking sheet*

1. In a bowl, combine flour, baking powder, and spices. Set aside.
2. In a mixing bowl, cream butter and sugar until light and fluffy. Add eggs 1 at a time, beating after each addition. Gradually add dry ingredients and extracts.
3. On a lightly floured surface, knead dough until smooth. Take pieces of dough the size of a medium egg and roll into 4-inch-long, ½-inch-thick ropes.
4. Shape ropes as noted in introduction, or use your imagination! Brush with egg glaze. Dip into dish filled with sesame seeds.
5. Place on lightly greased baking sheet. Bake in a preheated 350°F oven 15 to 20 minutes, or until golden brown. Cool on a wire rack.

NOTE: Store in an airtight container.

Halvah—Greek Easter Cake

Don't let the name fool you! This is not a sesame seed confection but a cake made of delightfully crunchy farina moistened with a sugar-and-cinnamon syrup. *Yields 1 cake*

> 1 *stick butter*
> 1 *cup granulated sugar*
> 3 *eggs*
> 1¾ *cups quick-cooking farina*
> 1¼ *cups blanched almonds, finely ground*
> ½ *tablespoon ground cinnamon*

Syrup
> 1 *cup granulated sugar*
> 2 *cups water*
> *1-inch cinnamon stick, broken*

> *2-cup mold*

1. In a mixing bowl, cream butter and sugar until light and fluffy. Add eggs 1 at a time, beating after each addition. Add remaining cake ingredients. Mix thoroughly.

2. Pour into greased mold. Bake in a preheated 350°F oven 35 to 40 minutes, or until a cake tester comes out clean.

3. While cake is baking, make syrup: Boil sugar, water, and cinnamon together until mixture is thick, about 10 minutes.

4. Before using syrup, discard cinnamon pieces. Remove cake from oven. Pour hot syrup over it. Cool cake in pan and cut.

Ma'Amoul—Lebanese Easter Cookies

(mah-mool)

These delicately crunchy cookies with their enticing walnut filling are an Easter treat from Lebanon. Orange-flower water and rose-water add to the charm of this exotic dessert. *Yields 3–3 1/2 dozen*

> 1 1/2 cups boiling water
> 3 cups farina
> 2 sticks butter, softened

> **Filling**
> 1/2 tablespoon orange-flower water *
> 1/2 tablespoon rosewater *
> 1/2 cup granulated sugar
> 3/4 cup finely chopped walnuts

> confectioners' sugar for coating

> baking sheet

1. Pour boiling water and farina in a mixing bowl. Mix until thickened. Add butter. Mix and allow to cool. Chill overnight.

2. To make filling, in a small bowl, combine orange-flower water, rosewater, sugar, and nuts. Mix thoroughly. Knead until smooth.

3. Make walnut-size balls. Place on greased baking sheet about 2 inches apart. Flatten with the tines of a fork.

4. Using thumb, make an indentation in each cookie. Put filling in indentations. Flatten filling.

5. Bake in a preheated 350°F oven 25 to 30 minutes, or until lightly browned. Cool on a wire rack. Dust with confectioners' sugar while warm and again before serving.

* Available in some gourmet shops, pharmacies, and suppliers of Middle Eastern foods.

Mämmi—Finnish Easter Rye Pudding

(MAM-me)

Mämmi is a dessert traditional in Finland for Easter. Orange peel and raisins give zest to the rye flour base of this unusual, and unusually delicious, pudding. Originally mämmi was baked in birch-bark baskets, but that practice has been outlawed in Finland to protect the trees. Finns are reported now to use a cardboard basket; I recommend a casserole dish. *Yields 6 servings*

> 2 *cups water*
> ⅓ *cup dark molasses*
> ⅛ *teaspoon salt*
> ⅔ *cup medium rye flour*
> 1 *tablespoon grated orange peel*
> ¼ *cup golden raisins*
> *sugar and light cream for serving*
>
> *1-quart casserole dish*

1. In a saucepan, combine water, molasses, salt, and 2 table-spoons of the flour. Bring to a slow boil, stirring constantly with a wire whisk. Remove from heat. Cover and let cool 1 hour.

2. Stir in remaining flour, orange peel, and raisins. Pour into greased casserole dish. Bake *uncovered* in a preheated 275°F oven 3 hours. Cool. To prevent drying out, cover tightly. Refrigerate.

NOTE: Serve with sugar and cream.

Whitepit Pudding

This milk pudding was traditional on Whit Tuesday in Somerset, England. A recipe for it has been in the same family for a century and a half. *Yields 6 to 8 servings*

> 4 cups milk
> ⅔ cup all-purpose flour
> 3 tablespoons dark molasses
> ⅓ cup granulated sugar
> 2 eggs
> 1 tablespoon butter
> ½ teaspoon ground cinnamon
> ¼ teaspoon ground allspice
> ¼ teaspoon ground cloves
>
> *1-quart soufflé dish*

1. In a mixing bowl, mix ¼ cup of the milk with flour to make a paste. In a saucepan, heat remaining milk to warm and add to paste. Stir.

2. Add molasses, sugar, eggs, butter, and spices. Mixture may now be curdled.

3. Pour into greased soufflé dish. Bake in a preheated 350°F oven about 1 hour, or until an inserted knife comes out clean. Chill and eat.

NOTE: Pudding may have a jelled bottom and a custardlike top.

Gaznates—Mexican Corpus Christi Fritters

(gahz-NAH-tays)

These sweet fritters are a post-Easter treat from Mexico. After participating in the religious celebration of the day, many Mexicans enjoy gaznates. *Yields 2 dozen*

> 1²/₃ *cups all-purpose flour*
> 7 *egg yolks*
> 1 *tablespoon butter*
> ¹/₃ *cup brandy*
> *oil for deep frying*
> 2 *tablespoons ground cinnamon for sprinkling on top*
> 1¼ *cups confectioners' sugar for sprinkling on top*
>
> *deep fryer or other deep pan for frying*

1. In a mixing bowl, combine flour, egg yolks, and butter. Mix. Add brandy. Mix thoroughly.

2. On a lightly floured surface, knead dough until smooth, about 5 minutes. Roll out dough to about ⅛-inch thickness. Cut into 3-inch squares. With each square, form a basket by pressing together two diagonally opposite corners. Moisten these touching corners to seal.

3. Heat oil to 375°F. Fry a few fritters at a time to golden brown, turning once. Remove and drain on paper towels. Combine cinnamon and sugar. Sprinkle on top of fritters.

Pennsylvania Dutch Coconut Easter Eggs

These candies make a delightful Easter treat, somewhat reminiscent of a Peter Paul Mounds candy bar. *Yields about 60*

> ¾ *cup unsalted mashed potato*
> 2 *cups coconut, fresh or dried*
> ½ *teaspoon salt*
> 1 *teaspoon vanilla extract*
> 3½ *cups confectioners' sugar*
> 8 *ounces semisweet chocolate*
> 1 *tablespoon vegetable oil*

1. In a mixing bowl, mix potato, coconut, salt, and vanilla. Gradually mix in sugar. Cover and refrigerate overnight.

2. Shape into ½-tablespoon-size eggs. Heat chocolate and oil until chocolate is melted. Dip eggs into chocolate-oil mixture. Set aside on wax paper in refrigerator to harden.

INDEPENDENCE DAY

JULY 4

Independence Day, the Fourth of July, is the chief nonreligious holiday in the United States. At first, many people expected the celebration to take place on July 2, the day in 1776 that the Continental Congress passed a resolution of independence. But the celebration was fixed instead on July 4, the day Congress adopted the document of the Declaration of Independence.

It was the earlier day that John Adams, later to become President, had in mind when he wrote his wife: "I am apt to believe that it will be celebrated by succeeding generations as the great anniversary festival. It ought to be commemorated as the day of deliverance, by solemn acts of devotion to God Almighty. It ought to be solemnized with pomp and pride, with shows, games and sports, guns, bells, bonfires and illuminations, from one end of this continent to the other, from this time forward, forevermore."

The next year in Philadelphia, such a celebration in fact filled the city with jubilation—on the Fourth. Bells rang throughout the day. Dignitaries of the city had a special dinner late in the afternoon, punctuated with toasts to the United States. At night, bonfires blazed in the streets and fireworks crackled. Candles gleamed from the windows of houses, providing what Adams called "the most splendid illumination I ever saw."

As the nation grew and spread, so did the celebration of Independence Day. The early festivities tended to be martial—with marching troops, military music, and salutes of cannons or gunfire. Communities across the nation now also emphasize pageants, sports events, and picnics, with fireworks at night. In general, the observance of Independence Day is remarkably similar to what Adams predicted—"with pomp and parade, with shows, games and sports, guns, bells, bonfires and illuminations. . . ."

The dessert here offers a personal way to join in the celebration of the nation's independence.

Strawberry Shortcake

Though strawberry shortcake is a treat that goes back three centuries in America, it is regarded in many areas of the United States as the perfect Independence Day dessert. *Yields 1 shortcake*

> 2 cups all-purpose flour
> 1 tablespoon baking powder
> 1/2 teaspoon salt
> 1/3 cup granulated sugar
> 1 teaspoon ground nutmeg
> 1 stick butter
> 2/3 cup milk
> 1/2 stick butter, melted
> 1 quart fresh strawberries
> 1 cup heavy cream, whipped
> sugar for sweetening
> 9-inch round cake pan

1. In a mixing bowl, combine flour, baking powder, salt, sugar, and nutmeg. Cut in 1 stick of butter with two knives or a pastry blender. Gradually add enough milk to make a soft dough.

2. Divide dough in half. * Pat or roll out 1/2 to fit in pan. Brush with 1/2 of melted butter. Place remaining dough in pan, shaped to fit.

* If you wish to make individual shortcakes, cut with a 3-inch cookie cutter.

3. Bake in a preheated 425°F oven 10 to 15 minutes, or until firm to the touch. Brush top with rest of melted butter. Remove from pan and slice horizontally.

4. Wash and hull strawberries. Crush slightly. Sweeten. Place ½ of berries on bottom half of cake. Top with second half of cake. Place remaining strawberries on top. Top with sweetened whipped cream.

13

SAINT OSWALD'S DAY

AUGUST 5

Oswald, king and saint, converted the people of Northumbria in England to Christianity. A song from the region goes:

> *By him upreared, the cross far threw*
> *Its shadows on Northumbrian sod,*
> *A folk that only idols knew*
> *Stretched forth its hand to God.*

Until his death in 642, Oswald spread the faith. Churches and monasteries long afterward bore testimony to his zeal. But even more powerful has been his legend. Until recent centuries, Saint Oswald was commemorated each year in many villages of northern England. Grasmere, however, has kept the tradition with remarkable purity, owing partly to the influence of the poet William Wordsworth.

The distinctive gingerbread here is a further local memorial to the much beloved saint.

Saint Oswald's Gingerbread

Children of Grasmere, in the Lake Country of England, traditionally strew rushes on the floor of their ancient village church on Saint Oswald's Day, the Saturday nearest August 5. In return, the children each receive a new penny and a piece of this orange-flavored gingerbread. *Yields about 6 dozen bars*

> 4 *cups flour*
> ½ *tablespoon baking soda*
> ½ *tablespoon cream of tartar*
> ½ *teaspoon salt*
> 1 *tablespoon ground ginger*
> 1 *tablespoon grated orange rind*
> 2 *sticks butter*
> ¾ *cup dark brown sugar, firmly packed*
> 1½ *teaspoons dark corn syrup*
> 6 *eggs*
> ¾ *cup candied orange peel, finely chopped*
>
> *9 × 13-inch pan*

1. Reserve 2 tablespoons of the flour. In a mixing bowl, combine flour, baking soda, cream of tartar, salt, ginger, and orange rind. Mix and set aside.

2. In a mixing bowl, cream butter and sugar until light and fluffy. Add corn syrup and then eggs 1 at a time, beating after each addition.

3. In a small mixing bowl, combine orange peel with reserved flour. Mix. Add to batter. Gradually add flour mixture.

4. Pour batter into greased pan. Bake in a preheated 350°F oven 30 to 40 minutes, or until a cake tester comes out clean. Cut into 1 by 2-inch bars while still warm.

14

SAINT ROCH'S DAY

AUGUST 16

Saint Roch, a French saint of the early fourteenth century, gave up all his goods when young and set out on a pilgrimage to Rome. Along the way, he stopped at hospitals to attend the sick. Stricken by the plague on his way home, Roch collapsed in a forest. There a dog visited him each day with a piece of bread. At last, the dog's master followed his pet into the forest, found Roch, and befriended him.

When Roch returned to his native town he was so worn out by years of suffering and self-deprivation that no one recognized him. Under suspicion of being a spy, he was thrown into prison, where he died. But devotion to Saint Roch grew over the years. He was especially remembered as a guardian against disease and pestilence. Artists often portrayed him with the dog that fed him in his time of need.

Saint Roch's Fingers

This concoction of ladyfingers and custard, a Spanish delicacy traditional in Saint Roch's honor, is a cool dessert just right for the doldrums of August. *Yields 4–6 servings*

> 2 *cups milk*
> 5 *egg yolks*
> 1/3 *cup granulated sugar*
> 1/4 *teaspoon salt*
> 1 *tablespoon cornstarch, if necessary*
> 2 *tablespoons brandy*
> *ladyfingers*
>
> *double boiler; glass serving dish*

1. In a saucepan, heat milk to hot without boiling. In a mixing bowl, combine egg yolks, sugar, and salt.
2. Put egg yolk mixture in double boiler. Without boiling, cook mixture until thick. (If mixture doesn't thicken, add cornstarch.)
3. Strain. Cool, and stir in brandy. Line bottom and sides of serving dish with ladyfingers (if necessary, shorten ladyfingers on sides). Pour cooled custard into dish. Chill.

15

ROSH HASHANAH

Rosh Hashanah, the Jewish New Year, literally means "beginning of the year." It falls on the first day of the Hebrew month of Tishri —usually in September—and ushers in a ten-day period of introspection, the Days of Awe, that culminates in the holiest day of the year for Jews, Yom Kippur, the Day of Atonement.

For thirty days before the New Year, the shofar (ram's horn) is blown in some synagogues to remind the congregation of the approaching High Holy Days of Rosh Hashanah and Yom Kippur. The shofar sounds again on Rosh Hashanah to warn the congregation to prepare for the judgment that will come on Yom Kippur. In the next ten days, all are supposed to cleanse away past sins and prepare to lead a better, more holy life. Jews use the occasion to exchange New Year's cards and to say to one another in Hebrew, "May you be inscribed [by God in the Book of Life] for a good New Year."

The foods eaten during Rosh Hashanah convey the themes of the holiday. "Eat of the fat and drink of the sweet," said the prophet Nehemiah. Fish, as a symbol of fruitfulness and abundance, is always served. Often the head of the fish goes to the head of the household in recognition of that person's leadership. The accompanying foods are traditionally rich and often sweet. Some families start the main meal with apples or round challah (symbolizing the cycle of the year) dipped in honey. Tzimmes, carrots and sometimes other vegetables and meat, sweetened with honey and stewed or baked, is a favorite dish.

Honey, standing for hopes of a sweet new year, appears prominently in the desserts for Rosh Hashanah. Lekach, a honey cake with raisins, chopped nuts, and spices, is justly one of the most renowned of these desserts. Teiglach, balls of dough boiled in honey and coated with nuts, is a confection cherished at this time. A variety of other desserts grace Rosh Hashanah tables.

Rosh Hashanah is a solemn festival, filled with reflection and plans for personal renewal. But the desserts traditional on this occasion hearten participants and delight those of other faiths.

Lekach—Honey Cake

(LEK-ak)

This cake is traditionally served on the first night of Rosh Hashanah. If not the earliest, it is at least one of the earliest sweet pastries ever made. The honey in it symbolizes hope for a sweet, or happy, new year. *Yields 1 cake*

> 5 *cups all-purpose flour*
> ½ *tablespoon baking powder*
> 1 *teaspoon baking soda*
> ½ *teaspoon ground cinnamon*
> ½ *teaspoon ground ginger*
> ½ *teaspoon ground allspice*
> 6 *eggs*
> 1 *cup honey*
> ½ *cup strong coffee*
> 1¾ *cups light brown sugar, firmly packed*
> ½ *cup vegetable oil*
> 1 *teaspoon vanilla extract*
> ½ *cup chopped dates*

$\frac{1}{4}$ *cup golden raisins*
$\frac{1}{4}$ *cup dark raisins*
$\frac{1}{2}$ *cup chopped toasted almonds*

10-inch tube pan

1. In a mixing bowl, combine $4\frac{1}{2}$ cups of the flour, baking powder, baking soda, and spices. Mix. Set aside.
2. In another mixing bowl, beat eggs, honey, coffee, brown sugar, oil, and vanilla. Gradually add flour mixture. Mix well.
3. In a small bowl, combine remaining flour with dates and raisins. Mix. Add this mixture and almonds to batter.
4. Pour batter into greased tube pan. Bake in a preheated 350°F oven 45 minutes. Lower heat to 300°F and bake 30 minutes more, or until a cake tester comes out clean. Cool in pan 10 minutes. Cool on a wire rack.

NOTE: Wait 24 hours before serving to allow honey flavor to develop.

Teiglach—Honey Balls

(TAYG-lakh)

A Rosh Hashanah favorite, these crisp honey-dipped balls are a classic treat either baked or fried. *Yields 6 cups*

4 *eggs*
1 *tablespoon granulated sugar*
3 *tablespoons vegetable oil*
2½ *cups all-purpose flour*
½ *tablespoon ground nutmeg*

Syrup
1½ *cups honey*
1½ *cups dark brown sugar, firmly packed*
½ *tablespoon ground ginger*
½ *tablespoon ground nutmeg*

⅓ *cup coarsely chopped walnuts for sprinkling on top*

baking sheet

1. In a mixing bowl, combine eggs, sugar, oil, flour, and nutmeg. Mix thoroughly. On a lightly floured surface, knead dough until smooth.
2. Divide dough into 6 pieces. Roll each piece into ½-inch-thick rope. Cut each rope into ½-inch lengths.
3. To make syrup: In a saucepan, boil honey, sugar, ginger, and nutmeg 5 minutes. Drop pieces of dough into syrup. Place dough on greased baking sheet.
4. Bake in a preheated 350°F oven about 25 minutes, or until dough starts to brown. Sprinkle chopped nuts on top. Resume baking 35 minutes. Remove from oven and place in a bowl. Serve.

NOTE: If well covered, will keep 2 weeks.

Rosh Hashanah Carrot Cake

The carrot in this rich moist cake emphasizes the theme of Rosh Hashanah. In Yiddish, the word for "carrot" also means "to increase"—a hope Jews share for a fruitful New Year. *Yields 1 cake*

3 cups all-purpose flour
½ tablespoon baking powder
½ teaspoon baking soda
¼ teaspoon salt
½ tablespoon ground cinnamon
1½ cups granulated sugar
1½ cups vegetable oil
3¼ cups grated carrots
4 eggs
⅔ cup coarsely chopped walnuts

Frosting
3-ounce package cream cheese
½ stick butter
1¾ cups confectioners' sugar
1 teaspoon lemon extract

10-inch Bundt pan

1. In a small mixing bowl, combine flour, baking powder, baking soda, salt, and cinnamon. Stir and set aside.
2. In a mixing bowl, mix sugar and oil. Add carrots. Stir. Add eggs 1 at a time, beating after each addition.
3. Gradually add flour mixture to batter. Mix. Fold in walnuts. Pour batter into greased Bundt pan.
4. Bake in a preheated 350°F oven 1 hour, or until a cake tester comes out clean. Cool on a wire rack.
5. To make frosting: In a bowl, combine frosting ingredients. Mix. Frost cake when it is cool.

Rosh Hashanah Sponge Cake

This delicate flavorful sponge cake, with a hint of lemon, is a cherished Rosh Hashanah treat. *Yields 1 cake*

> 6 *eggs, separated*
> 1 1/4 *cups granulated sugar*
> 1/4 *cup lemon juice*
> 1 *tablespoon grated lemon rind*
> 1 1/4 *cups all-purpose flour*
> 1/2 *teaspoon salt*
> 1/2 *tablespoon baking powder*
>
> *10-inch tube pan*

1. In a mixing bowl, beat egg yolks until light and fluffy. Add sugar, lemon juice, and lemon rind. Mix.
2. In a small bowl, combine flour, salt, and baking powder. Gradually add to batter.
3. Beat egg whites until stiff peaks stand up. Fold into cake batter.
4. Pour into ungreased tube pan. Bake in a preheated 350°F oven 50 to 60 minutes, or until the cake springs back when lightly touched. Invert pan over a wire rack. Allow cake to cool.

16

SUKKOT—FEAST OF TABERNACLES

This joyous holiday is also known as the Feast of Booths. During the holiday Jews recall the journey of their ancestors across the wilderness with Moses leading. Falling in the week after Yom Kippur, in September or October, the holiday also celebrates the fall harvest.

The Hebrew name of the holiday, Sukkot, is the plural of *sukkah*, the booth or temporary home the ancient Israelite farmer built in his field during the harvest. To commemorate that time, an observant Jewish family today erects a sukkah outside the home or shares one built by the community. The booth is roofed with green branches, with openings left to the sky. Fruits, gourds, and festive homemade decorations are hung inside. The observant Jewish family eats meals in the booth through the nine days of the holiday.

On each of the first seven mornings of the Feast of Tabernacles, except Saturday, observant households conduct a special ceremony with a *lulav*—a willow branch and a palm branch bound with myrtle—probably a reminder of the harvest, and an *etrog*—a citrus fruit from Israel. Simchath Torah, the Rejoicing over the Torah (scroll of the Pentateuch), falls on the ninth and last day of the holiday. In this ceremony, the Torah is carried in joyful procession in the synagogue or temple.

As an expression of happiness, many Jews wear holiday clothes during the Feast of the Tabernacles. They prepare elaborate meals, often preceded by a blessing spoken over a piece of bread dipped in honey.

Apple Strudel I

What could be more appropriate for the fall harvest than an apple dessert? This strudel is a universal favorite. *Yields 2 strudels*

> 2 cups all-purpose flour
> 1 teaspoon baking powder
> ½ teaspoon salt
> 1 tablespoon granulated sugar
> 1 egg
> 2½ tablespoons vegetable oil
> 1½–2⅓ cups ice water

Filling
> 2 cups tart apples, peeled, cored, and sliced
> 4 tablespoons candied orange peel, finely chopped
> ⅓ cup golden raisins
> 1 teaspoon ground cinnamon
> 1 teaspoon grated orange rind
> ½ cup granulated sugar
> ½ cup finely ground bread crumbs
> ⅓ cup shredded coconut (optional)
> ½ blanched almonds, coarsely chopped

> 2 tablespoons oil for brushing
> confectioners' sugar for sprinkling on top

> baking sheet

1. In a mixing bowl, combine flour, baking powder, salt, and sugar. Make a well in the center of the flour. Add egg and oil. Mix thoroughly. Gradually add ice water until dough is soft but not sticky.
2. On a lightly floured surface, knead dough until smooth, about 2 minutes. Cover with an inverted bowl 30 minutes.
3. Divide dough in half. Roll each half out as thin as possible into an 18 by 6-inch rectangle.

4. To make filling: In a bowl, combine filling ingredients. Mix.

5. Place ½ of filling in the center of the rectangle of dough. Using scissors, make 2-inch cuts every 1 inch on long sides of rectangle. Crisscross strips on top of filling. Place on greased baking sheet. Repeat for second strudel.

6. Brush tops with oil. Bake in a preheated 350°F oven 35 to 40 minutes, or until crisp and brown. Cool on a wire rack. Sprinkle with confectioners' sugar just before serving.

Apple Strudel II (Phyllo Dough)

This apple strudel is much like the previous one, but the phyllo dough makes it a flakier pastry. *Yields 2 strudels*

> 6 *tart apples, peeled, cored, and sliced*
> ½ *cup finely ground walnuts*
> 2 *teaspoons ground cinnamon*
> 2 *tablespoons lemon juice*
> ⅔ *cup granulated sugar*
> 6 *sheets phyllo dough*
> 1 *stick butter, melted*
> ⅓ *cup finely ground bread crumbs*
> *confectioners' sugar for sprinkling on top*
>
> *baking sheet*

1. To make filling: In a mixing bowl, combine apples, walnuts, cinnamon, lemon juice, and sugar. Toss and set aside.

2. Unfold phyllo dough sheets. To prevent drying, cover with a damp cloth. Place a phyllo dough sheet on a work surface. Brush with melted butter. Repeat 2 more times.

3. Place ½ of filling down the center of prepared phyllo dough. Fold in thirds. Fold ends over. Pinch seams. Turn over. Brush top with butter. Make 3 or 4 diagonal slashes with a sharp knife. Repeat to make second strudel.

4. Place on greased baking sheet. Bake in a preheated 350°F oven 35 to 40 minutes, or until golden brown. Sprinkle with confectioners' sugar just before serving.

Apple Torte

This torte, almost a coffee cake in texture, beautifully carries out the harvest theme of Sukkot. *Yields 1 torte*

> 2 cups all-purpose flour
> ½ tablespoon baking powder
> ⅛ teaspoon salt
> 3 tablespoons granulated sugar
> 1 tablespoon grated lemon rind
> ⅓ cup shortening
> 3 eggs
> 1 tablespoon lemon juice

Filling
> 4 cups green apples, peeled and coarsely grated
> ½ cup granulated sugar
> ½ tablespoon ground cinnamon
> ½ tablespoon grated lemon rind
> 2 tablespoons finely ground bread crumbs
> ¼ cup almonds, finely chopped
>
> egg white for brushing top
> 2 tablespoons granulated sugar for sprinkling on top
> 1 tablespoon ground cinnamon for sprinkling on top
>
> 8-inch springform pan

1. In a mixing bowl, combine flour, baking powder, salt, sugar, lemon rind, and shortening. Mix. Add eggs and lemon juice. Mix thoroughly. Cover and set aside.

2. In a mixing bowl, combine apples, sugar, cinnamon, and lemon rind. Mix and set aside.

3. Divide dough in half. Roll out ½ of dough to ⅛-inch thickness. Place in greased pan. Sprinkle bread crumbs on top. Add apple mixture. Sprinkle almonds over top.

4. Roll out remaining dough. Place on top of apple mixture. Make a few cuts to allow steam to escape. Brush with egg white. In a cup, combine sugar and cinnamon. Sprinkle mixture on top.

5. Bake in a preheated 400°F oven 30 minutes. Lower heat to 350°F and bake 30 minutes more, or until evenly brown. Cool on a wire rack.

17

HALLOWEEN

OCTOBER 31

For costumed children passing from house to house, imagine instead spirits wandering eerily abroad. For "trick or treat," imagine the ritual burning of those failing to supply pagan priests with wood for their bonfires. For the modern bonfire, imagine a *bone*-fire with actual bones crackling in the flames. Most modern Halloween customs derive from the Celtic festival of the dead once celebrated throughout the British Isles.

The Celts called their festival Samhain (SAH-win). Taking place on November 1, it was the major holiday of the Celtic year and marked the beginning of their winter. Celtic priests, the Druids, led the people in sacrifices of animals and offerings of vegetables and fruits. Entire communities lit sacred fires on hilltops the night before Samhain. They then lit their hearth fires anew with coals from the bonfires as a symbol of religious renewal for the coming year.

Ever present in the minds of the worshipers was the large number of mysterious forces in nature that had to be appeased. Especially remembered were the people who had died during the year. The Celts sought to speed these souls on their way by leaving out food and drink to sustain them on their trip to the underworld.

Christian missionaries found Samhain to be a serious stumbling block in their campaign to convert the Celts. Customs hallowed by centuries of devotion were not readily abandoned by farming people who felt the need for divine help to survive weather and circumstance. In 601, Pope Gregory I (the Great) instructed missionaries to coopt pagan customs by assimilating them to Christian practice. About a century later, this policy led to the designation of November 1 as All Saints' Day, a feast day that honored all Christian saints. The day was also known as All Hallows' Day—"hallow" being another name for saint.

The old beliefs never wholly died out. Halloween (short for All Hallow Even[ing]) still carried for the people of the British Isles, and others sharing their traditions, overtones of an extinct religion. The associations with the dead and their journey to the afterlife dimly persist. Additions such as the jack-o'-lantern harmonize with the older traditions. The Irish developed the custom of placing a candle inside a hollowed and carved turnip and using this skull-like lantern to light their way from house to house on Halloween. Witches, bats, and other creatures real or imaginary that came to be associated with Halloween similarly hint at the holiday's dark past.

Fortunately, Halloween has always had a festive side. These recipes will help make a party of the holiday and remind us that the ancient Celts enjoyed Halloween even as they used the occasion to communicate with the dead.

Pumpkin Cookies

These soft cookies offer true pumpkin flavor—just right for a Halloween gift or snack. *Yields about 3–4 dozen*

> 1 stick butter
> ¾ cup light brown sugar, firmly packed
> 1 cup canned pumpkin
> 1 egg
> 1 teaspoon vanilla extract
> 1 teaspoon baking powder
> ½ teaspoon salt
> 1 tablespoon ground cinnamon
> ½ teaspoon ground nutmeg
> ½ teaspoon ground allspice
> 2½ cups all-purpose flour
> ½ cup dark raisins (optional)
> ½ cup chopped walnuts (optional)
>
> baking sheet

1. In a mixing bowl, cream butter and sugar until light and fluffy. Add pumpkin, egg, and vanilla. Mix thoroughly.
2. In a small bowl, combine baking powder, salt, spices, and flour. Gradually add to pumpkin mixture. Mix thoroughly.
3. If desired, stir in raisins and/or walnuts. Drop 1 tablespoon of dough on greased baking sheet. Bake in a preheated 350°F oven 10 to 15 minutes, or until lightly browned. Cool on a wire rack.

Scottish Halloween Cake

This white cake—a tradition in Scotland—is covered with an orange frosting decorated with Halloween figures such as witches on broomsticks, black cats, and bats. The Scots often include little charms in the cake revealing the fortunes of those who find them —a button for those who will stay single (at least for the coming year), a ring for marriage, and a horseshoe for good luck. *Yields 1 cake*

2 *sticks butter*
¾ *cup granulated sugar*
6 *eggs*
3 *cups self-rising flour*
1 *tablespoon grated orange rind*
¼ *cup milk*
apricot jam (for between layers)

Icing
1 *box confectioners' sugar*
1 *cup butter*
¼ *cup orange juice*
orange food coloring
water, if necessary

Decorations
4 *ounces semisweet chocolate*
1 *ounce bitter chocolate*

2 *8-inch round cake pans;*
cake plate; double boiler

1. In a mixing bowl, cream butter and sugar until light and fluffy. Add eggs 1 at a time, beating after each addition.

2. Add flour, orange rind, and milk. Mix. Pour ½ of batter into each greased and floured cake pan. Bake in a preheated 350°F

oven 25 to 35 minutes, or until a cake tester comes out clean. Cool on a wire rack.

3. Slice each layer in half horizontally. Place on cake plate. Spread apricot jam between each layer.

4. To make icing: In a mixing bowl, combine confectioners' sugar, butter, orange juice, and food coloring. Mix thoroughly. Add water if necessary for spreading consistency. Ice the cake.

5. To make chocolate silhouette: Melt the two chocolates together in double boiler. Make a paper cone out of wax or parchment paper. After chocolate cools slightly, cut tip of cone and outline silhouettes on wax paper. Fill in silhouettes. Let harden. (To speed up hardening, place in refrigerator or freezer.) Peel off wax paper. Decorate top and/or sides of cake.

18

ALL SOULS' DAY

NOVEMBER 2

Have mercy on all Christian Soules
For a Soule-cake!

The customs that make All Souls' Day so strangely festive and somber go back to the early centuries of Christianity and even to the paleolithic traditions of the Celtic people. As noted in the preceding chapter on Halloween, Christian missionaries faced special problems in converting the Celts. The missionaries tried unsuccessfully to substitute All Saints' Day, November 1, for Samhain, their Celtic festival of the dead.

Four centuries later, the Church established All Souls' Day, November 2, partly to Christianize the season further. On this day the faithful were supposed to attend mass and pray for souls in purgatory. All Souls', however, ironically reinforced the widespread pagan belief that the dead returned to their earthly homes at this time of year. People often simply continued their ancient customs such as leaving out food and drink for the returning dead.

In England, "soulers" traditionally walked along the streets on All Souls' Day singing a song like the one quoted from. Soul cakes specifically baked for the occasion were given to them (for recipe see *The Festive Bread Book*). But in many parts of Britain, other foods and even money came to be substituted for the cakes. France, Italy, Switzerland, and other European countries maintained similar traditions of their own.

Mexico today offers the most exuberant All Souls' Day celebration anywhere. Drawing heavily on Aztec traditions as well as on Christianity, the Mexicans celebrate the day with colorful songs, poems, processions, and foods with the theme of death. Families erect altars at graveside and offer special foods for dead relatives. Amid exploding fireworks, the participants remember their beloved dead with gravity and joy.

These recipes, from several countries, are delectable reminders of All Souls' Day. In them, the joyful side of the day predominates over the spooky traditions long associated with All Souls'.

Fave dei Morte—Beans of the Dead

(FAH-vay dee MOR-tay)

Colorful pageants take place throughout Italy on All Souls' Day, and children eagerly await treats such as the almond-flavored, bean-shaped cookies here. *Yields 5½ dozen 2-inch-long cookies*

> 1 *stick butter*
> ¾ *cup granulated sugar*
> 1¼ *cups almonds, finely ground*
> 1 *egg*
> ½ *cup all-purpose flour*
> 2 *tablespoons grated lemon rind*
>
> *baking sheet*

1. In a mixing bowl, cream butter and sugar together until light and fluffy. Add almonds, egg, flour, and lemon rind. Beat thoroughly.

2. Cover bowl, chill dough overnight.

3. Break off walnut-size pieces of dough. Shape like kidney beans

4. Place on lightly greased baking sheet. Bake in a preheated 350°F oven 15 to 20 minutes, or until light brown. Leave on baking sheet about 10 minutes; then cool on a wire rack.

Dry Bones Cookies

These All Souls' cookies are a Swiss delicacy. Despite their grim name, they have a crunchy texture redolent of almonds and rose-water. *Yields 4½ dozen*

> 1 stick butter
> ¾ cup granulated sugar
> 1 teaspoon ground cinnamon
> 3 eggs
> 1 tablespoon rosewater
> 2¾–3 cups all-purpose flour
> ¼ teaspoon salt
> 1½ cups almonds, coarsely chopped
> 1 egg yolk beaten with 1 tablespoon water for glaze
>
> baking sheet

1. In a mixing bowl, cream butter, sugar, and cinnamon until light and fluffy. Add eggs 1 at a time, beating after each addition.
2. Add rosewater, 2½ cups of the flour, and salt. Mix. If dough is too sticky, add more flour gradually.
3. On a lightly floured surface, knead in ground almonds. *Chill dough overnight.*
4. Shape dough into 2½-inch rolls (bones). Brush with egg glaze. Place on lightly greased baking sheet.
5. Bake in a preheated 350°F oven 10 to 15 minutes, or until golden brown. Cool on baking sheet 2 minutes; then cool on a wire rack.

NOTE: Store in an airtight container.

19

GUY FAWKES DAY

NOVEMBER 5

Please to remember the fifth of November
Gunpowder, treason, and plot;
I see no reason why gunpowder treason
Should ever be forgot.

So sing English children on Guy Fawkes Day—a curious case of a holiday based on a desperate plot followed by horrible consequences. Guy Fawkes (1570–1606), a Roman Catholic convert, was recruited by Catholic conspirators in 1604 in a plot against King James I. Under James, thousands of Catholics had been executed because of their religious beliefs. Furthermore, James was known to be planning to exile Catholic priests. The conspirators decided to strike back both at James and at Parliament, which was also anti-Catholic.

The conspirators rented a cellar that reached under the Parliament buildings. They stored thirty-six barrels of gunpowder in the cellar along with iron bars and stones to serve as shrapnel. When James opened Parliament on November 5, 1605, the conspirators planned to blow him up along with the members of Parliament.

The plot was discovered and Fawkes was seized. Tortured on the rack, he confessed and implicated other conspirators. He and three others were tried, found guilty, and hanged. Relieved at averting a national disaster, Parliament designated November 5 as a permanent day of thanksgiving.

Children celebrate Guy Fawkes Day by constructing rag doll effigies of Fawkes ("guys") and displaying them on the street with the demand, "A penny for the guy!" Fireworks crackle and bonfires blaze at night. Some places have torchlight processions and parades with marching bands. "Anti-popery" is no longer a common theme in these celebrations.

You will find here traditional Guy Fawkes Day desserts—
gentle reminders of one of the more lurid chapters in English
history.

Parkin

In some parts of England, this plain oatmeal cake is so popular on
Guy Fawkes Day that the celebration is called Parkin Day. Traditionally, Yorkshire folk munched Parkin and drank hot milk at
the bonfires lighted at night. If the cake seems a little too plain,
try putting jam on it. *Yields about 5 dozen bars*

> 3 cups all-purpose flour
> ½ teaspoon baking soda
> ½ tablespoon baking powder
> 2 teaspoons ground ginger
> 1¾ cups finely ground oatmeal
> 1 stick butter
> ⅔ cup granulated sugar
> ⅓ cup dark molasses
> 3 eggs
> ⅔ cup milk
>
> *9 × 13-inch pan*

1. In a bowl, combine flour, baking soda, baking powder,
ginger, and oatmeal. Mix and set aside.
2. In a mixing bowl, cream butter and sugar until light and
fluffy. Add molasses and eggs. Mix. To batter mixture gradually
add flour mixture alternately with milk.
3. Grease pan and pour in batter. Bake in a preheated 350°F
oven 30 to 35 minutes, or until a cake tester comes out clean. Cut
into 2 by 1-inch bars.

Parkin Fingers

These tangy cookies, topped with lemon frosting, are a great favorite in Britain on Guy Fawkes Day. People like to munch on them after strenuously denouncing the ringleader of the Gunpowder Plot. *Yields about 4½ dozen*

3½   cups all-purpose flour
½   teaspoon baking soda
¼   teaspoon salt
1   tablespoon grated lemon rind
1½   sticks butter
⅔   cup light brown sugar, firmly packed
2   eggs
⅔   cup light molasses
1½   cups sour cream

Icing
1   stick butter
2   cups confectioners' sugar
1   tablespoon lemon juice

9 × 13-inch pan

1. In a mixing bowl, combine flour, baking soda, salt, and lemon rind. Add butter and brown sugar. Mix.
2. Add eggs, molasses, and sour cream. Mix thoroughly.
3. Place in lightly greased and floured pan. Bake in a preheated 350°F oven 25 to 30 minutes, or until a cake tester comes out clean. Cool about 10 minutes in pan. Remove and cool on a wire rack.
4. For icing, mix butter, sugar, and lemon juice. Spread on top of cooled cake. Cut into 1 by 2-inch fingers.

Queen's Pudding

After the bonfires and the burning of an effigy, the British often celebrate Guy Fawkes Day with a late supper. A vegetable soup is followed by a chicken or meat pie. Then comes a dessert that for many caps this day of horseplay and hilarity—Queen's Pudding. This custard dessert is served warm from the oven, topped with raspberry jam and meringue—a charming finish to one of Britain's quaintest celebrations. *Yields 6–8 servings*

> 1 *cup soft white bread crumbs*
> 1 *tablespoon vanilla sugar (see page 5)*
> 1 *tablespoon grated lemon rind*
> 1⅔ *cups milk*
> 3 *eggs*
> 3 *tablespoons raspberry jam*
> 1 *tablespoon water*
> 1 *tablespoon granulated sugar plus sugar for sprinkling on top*
>
> *8 × 8-inch ovenproof dish*

1. In a large mixing bowl, combine bread crumbs, vanilla sugar, and lemon rind. In a saucepan, heat milk to warm (not hot). Add to mixture. Stir thoroughly. Let sit 10 minutes.

2. Lightly grease ovenproof dish. Separate eggs; add yolks to mixture. Reserve whites for meringue. Pour mixture into dish.

3. Bake in a preheated 325°F oven 20 to 25 minutes, or until firm enough so jam can be spread on it.

4. Lower heat to 250°F. Combine raspberry jam and water; mix. Spread jam over custard.

5. Beat egg whites until stiff peaks stand up. Fold in 1 tablespoon of sugar. Lightly spread over custard and jam. Sprinkle lightly with sugar.

6. Bake about 20 minutes, or until meringue is lightly brown and firm. Serve hot or cold with cream.

20

SAINT MARTIN'S DAY

NOVEMBER 11

Even before becoming a Christian, Martin showed purity of soul by giving his cloak to a beggar. His holy deeds after conversion brought him devotion and unwanted fame. He built himself a hermitage so he could worship undisturbed. Nevertheless, in 371 he was acclaimed bishop of Tours.

Saint Martin became patron of winegrowers and tavern keepers. Because of the gift of his cloak, he was patron of beggars. In parts of Europe, children sought treats door to door on Saint Martin's Day in commemoration of his role as the beggar's guardian.

So renowned was Saint Martin that a spell of mild weather (Indian summer) around mid-November became known as Saint Martin's summer. But however mild the weather at this time of year, snow is usually not far away, so people felt that Saint Martin might arrive on his horse in a flurry of snow. Almond cookies, Saint Martin's Horseshoes, are baked so that his horse will be properly shod.

Saint Martin's Horseshoes

In parts of Europe, children are told that fourth-century Saint Martin arrives November 11 on a snow-white horse. In his honor, they are given these horseshoe cookies whose almondy flavor makes them universally popular. *Yields 2–3 dozen*

> 2 *sticks butter*
> ⅓ *cup granulated sugar*
> 2 *cups all-purpose flour*
> ¾ *cup unblanched almonds, finely ground*
> 1 *teaspoon almond extract*
> 1 *teaspoon grated lemon peel*
> *confectioners' sugar for coating*
>
> *baking sheet*

1. In a mixing bowl, cream butter and sugar until light and fluffy. Gradually add flour and almonds. Add almond extract and lemon peel. Mix thoroughly.

2. Roll out dough to ½-inch thickness. Cut 3-inch ropes and shape into horseshoes. Place on lightly greased baking sheet.

3. Bake in a preheated 300°F oven about 15 to 20 minutes, or until light brown.

4. Remove from baking sheet with spatula under curved side (other side breaks). Cool on a wire rack.

NOTE: Before serving, roll in confectioners' sugar.

21

THANKSGIVING

LAST THURSDAY IN NOVEMBER

Our harvest being gotten in, our governor sent four men on fowling, that we might after a special manner rejoice together after we had gathered the fruit of our labors. The four in one day killed as much fowl as, with a little help beside, served the company almost a week. At which time, amongst other recreations, we exercised our arms, many of the Indians coming amongst us, and among the rest their greatest king Massasoit, with some ninety men, whom for three days we entertained and feasted, and they went out and killed five deer, which they brought to the plantation and bestowed on our governor, and upon the captain and others.

Edward Winslow's brief description of the nation's first Thanksgiving, in 1621, is the only eyewitness account of that historical event. We are left in the dark as to exactly what the Pilgrims did on that occasion and what they ate. Yet historians have reconstructed the festivities in the light of traditions the Pilgrims brought with them from the Old World and foods available to them in the New World.

The first Thanksgiving was not primarily a religious occasion. That would have been celebrated with fasting, praying, and many hours at worship in church. In fact, the first Thanksgiving was a New World version of Harvest Home, an agricultural holiday that took place in England after completion of the harvest. It was celebrated with feasting, dancing, and games.

What did the pilgrims eat at their party? They lacked the wheat or rye flour for making pie crust, and they had no sugar.

But as compensation, the Pilgrims had a rich supply of foods native to the New World—wild turkey, venison (an aristocratic treat in England), fish of various kinds, pumpkins, berries, and corn.

James Deetz, an archaeologist who helped direct Plimoth Plantation at Plymouth, Massachusetts, and Jay Anderson, an authority on ethnic foods, have suggested the following menu as one the Pilgrims might well have eaten at the first Thanksgiving:

Roast Goose
Venison
Stewed Pumpkin (as a vegetable)
Frumenty
Ale   Corn Cakes

Frumenty, the dessert, was a pudding long popular at Harvest Home. For the Pilgrims, its ingredients would have included cornmeal, water, spices, and wild fruits. (Milk would not have been available to the Pilgrims at the first Thanksgiving unless goats had come over on the *Mayflower,* for which there is no evidence.)

Two years after the first Thanksgiving, the Pilgrims gave the holiday a more religious cast by emphasizing prayers offering thanks for the year's blessings. Yet the occasion remained festive, with feasting and amusements as part of the celebration. Pumpkin pie took over from frumenty as the dessert most characteristic of Thanksgiving. Indian pudding, though enjoyed at other times, also became a favorite Thanksgiving treat.

In 1863, President Abraham Lincoln made Thanksgiving Day a national holiday. Thanksgiving took its place as one of the most revered and widely celebrated holidays throughout the nation—a time for rejoicing and feasting.

Pumpkin Pie

It is not known for sure, but the pilgrims may have first received pumpkins from the Indians. This colorful vegetable became a staple food—sometimes simply boiled, sometimes cooked with other ingredients to form more complex treats such as pumpkin pie. This recipe is a favorite family version of this centuries-old Thanksgiving dessert. *Yields 9-inch pie*

> 1 *egg, beaten*
> 1/3 *cup granulated sugar*
> 1/3 *cup molasses*
> 1/2 *teaspoon salt*
> 1/2 *teaspoon ground cinnamon*
> 1/2 *teaspoon ground ginger*
> 1 *cup canned pumpkin*
> 2 *cups milk*
> *unbaked 9-inch pie crust*
> *ground nutmeg*
>
> *9-inch pie plate*

1. In a mixing bowl, combine egg, sugar, molasses, salt, cinnamon, ginger, and pumpkin. Mix. Add milk; mix thoroughly.
2. Pour into pie crust. Dust top with nutmeg. Bake in a preheated 400°F oven 15 minutes. Then lower heat to 350°F and bake 35 to 40 minutes, or until done. (Test by inserting a knife. When knife comes out clean, the pie is done.)

Indian Pudding

This Colonial American dish, simply made but fragrant and nourishing, received its name not because the Indians originated it but because of the Indian corn that gives it body. It is one of the oldest New England traditions for Thanksgiving. *Yields 6–8 servings*

3 *cups milk*
⅓ *cup cornmeal*
½ *teaspoon salt*
2 *eggs, beaten*
¼ *cup granulated sugar*
⅓ *cup dark molasses*
½ *teaspoon ground ginger*
½ *teaspoon ground cinnamon*

1-quart casserole dish

1. In a saucepan, combine milk, cornmeal, and salt. Boil, stirring constantly, about 10 minutes.
2. In a large bowl, combine remaining ingredients. Gradually add cornmeal mixture, beating until smooth.
3. Place in greased casserole dish. Bake in a preheated 300°F oven about 1½ hours.

NOTE: If you use a Crockpot, lightly grease. Turn on high 15 minutes. Put pudding in Crockpot; cover. Cook 2 to 3 hours, or set on low 6 to 8 hours.

Shaker Thanksgiving Cake

Typical of Shaker craftsmanship in its simple elegance, this cake will grace any Thanksgiving table. *Yields 2 cakes*

> 3 cups all-purpose flour
> 1 tablespoon baking powder
> 2 sticks butter
> 1½ cups granulated sugar
> ¾ cup milk
> 2 cups hickory nuts or walnuts, coarsely chopped
> 6 egg whites, beaten stiff
>
> 2 Bundt pans or tube pans

1. In a bowl, combine flour and baking powder. Set aside. In a mixing bowl, cream butter and sugar until light and fluffy.
2. Alternately add dry ingredients and milk to butter mixture. Add nuts and stir. Fold in egg whites. Pour into greased pans.
3. Bake in a preheated 350°F oven 45 to 55 minutes, or until a cake tester comes out clean. Cool on a wire rack.

NOTE: Allow to mellow several weeks for best flavor.

22

SAINT BARBARA'S DAY

DECEMBER 4

In the third century, Saint Barbara's rich father Dioscorus confined his daughter in a tower to protect the girl from all harmful influences. While there, Barbara became converted to Christianity. Dioscorus, a fanatical pagan, turned her over to the authorities, but torture failed to cause Barbara to forswear Christ. In a blind fury, Barbara's father then personally beheaded her. A bolt of lightning struck Dioscorus and fire consumed him.

For more than a thousand years, the legend of Saint Barbara served as solace, especially for those in danger from fire or storms. She was also, curiously, regarded as the protector of miners and artillerymen. Saint Barbara has been dropped from the church calendar because her story cannot be substantiated, but there are those who still remember her.

Saint Barbara's Wheat Pudding

This nourishing mixture of whole grain wheat, honey, nuts, and fruits is served in Lebanon and Syria to commemorate Saint Barbara. *Yields 6–8 servings*

Pudding
1¼ *cups whole grain wheat*
4 *cups water*
½ *teaspoon salt*
⅓ *cup golden raisins*
½ *cup blanched slivered almonds*
½ *cup coarsely chopped walnuts*
½ *cup pine nuts*
⅓ *cup granulated sugar*
¼ *cup honey*
½ *cup mixed candied fruit peel*
½ *teaspoon rosewater* *
½ *teaspoon orange-flower water* *

Topping
ground cinnamon
granulated sugar
chopped walnuts
chopped slivered almonds

large serving bowl

* Available in some gourmet shops, pharmacies, and suppliers of Middle Eastern foods.

1. Rinse whole grain wheat with boiling water. Place in a saucepan and cover with 4 cups of boiling water. Cover and simmer 3 to 4 hours, until grains are tender. If necessary, add more boiling water. Water should be absorbed when grain is done. Pour off excess water.

2. Add salt, raisins, nuts, sugar, honey, mixed fruit peel, rosewater, and orange-flower water. Stir until thick and moist and sugar is dissolved. Place in large serving bowl. Chill thoroughly. Serve with toppings chosen from those listed.

23

EVE OF SAINT NICHOLAS

DECEMBER 5

The Eve of Saint Nicholas is a time of jollity and feasting in northern European countries. This holiday honors a saint believed to have been a bishop in fourth-century Asia Minor. Amost nothing is known about his life, but he is said to have performed many good deeds such as furnishing gold coins to poor girls for their dowry. Travelers, sailors, bakers, and children have claimed Saint Nicholas as their patron saint.

In Holland, Saint Nicholas' Eve and feast day have long enjoyed immense popularity. By the thirteenth century, the people of Holland had built twenty-three churches in his name. The Dutch still celebrate the Eve and day of Saint Nicholas with pageantry, presents, and sweetmeats. In mid-November, *Sinterklaas,* as the saint is known, arrives from Spain in a steamboat. After riding through Amsterdam on a white horse and being greeted by thousands of children, he waits for the evening of his celebration. Then he and his Moorish helper, Black Peter, leave cookies, cakes, and other treats for the children.

The Dutch brought the story of Saint Nicholas to America. The name Santa Claus itself comes from *Sinterklaas.* It is fitting that these desserts also come from Holland, preserver of so much Saint Nicholas lore.

Jan Hagel—Dutch Cinnamon Cookies

(YAWN HAWG-el)

These cookies, delicately flavored with cinnamon and walnuts, are a classic Saint Nicholas' Eve treat in Holland. *Yields about 4 dozen*

2 *sticks butter*
3/4 *cup granulated sugar*
1 *egg*
2 *cups all-purpose flour*
1/4 *teaspoon salt*
1 *egg yolk beaten with 1 tablespoon water for glaze*

Topping
1/4 *cup granulated sugar*
1 *teaspoon ground cinnamon*
1/2 *cup finely chopped walnuts*

15½ × 10½ × *1-inch jelly-roll pan*

1. In a mixing bowl, cream butter and sugar until light and fluffy. Add egg. Gradually add flour and salt. Mix thoroughly.
2. Spread batter in lightly greased jelly-roll pan. Brush batter with egg glaze.
3. In a small bowl, combine sugar and cinnamon; sprinkle on top of glaze. Sprinkle nuts on top.
4. Bake in a preheated 350°F oven 15 to 20 minutes, or until golden brown. Cut while warm into 3 by 1-inch bars. Cool on a wire rack.

Speculaas—Saint Nicholas Cookies

(SPECK-oo-laws)

Among the treats the Dutch offer on Saint Nicholas' Eve are speculaas, the fragrant spice cookies here. *Yields about 6 dozen*

⅔ *cup light brown sugar, firmly packed*
¼ *cup milk*
2½ *cups flour*
½ *teaspoon ground ginger*
½ *teaspoon ground nutmeg*
1 *teaspoon ground cloves*
1 *teaspoon ground cinnamon*
¼ *teaspoon baking powder*
¼ *teaspoon salt*
2 *sticks butter*
¼ *cup slivered almonds, finely ground*

springerle rolling pin; baking sheet

1. In a small mixing bowl, mix sugar and milk thoroughly. In a large mixing bowl, combine flour, spices, baking powder, and salt.

2. Using a pastry blender, cut butter into flour mixture until of cornmeal consistency.

3. Add sugar mixture and almonds. Knead dough until smooth, about 3 to 5 minutes. Place in a bowl or wrap in foil. Refrigerate overnight.

4. On a lightly floured surface, roll out dough to ¼-inch thickness. Then stamp out patterns with springerle cookie rolling pin. Cut and place on lightly greased baking sheet.

5. Bake in a preheated 350°F oven about 15 minutes, or until golden brown. Cool on a wire rack.

NOTE: Make about 2 weeks ahead of time. Store in an airtight container.

Banketletter—Saint Nicholas Pastry Letter

(BAWN-ket-LET-ter)

On Saint Nicholas' Eve, good Dutch children each receive one of these almond-filled cookies shaped like the initial letters of their first names. *Yields about 1 dozen*

>2 *cups flour*
>½ *teaspoon salt*
>1½ *sticks butter*
>¼–⅓ *cup ice water*
>2 *cups almond paste (see page 4)*
>1 *egg yolk beaten with 1 tablespoon water for glaze*
>
>*baking sheet*

1. In a mixing bowl, combine flour, salt, and butter. Add water 1 tablespoon at a time, until dough can be shaped into a ball. Cover and refrigerate 1 hour.

2. Make almond paste.

3. On a lightly floured surface, roll out dough to ¼-inch thickness. With a sharp knife, cut 2½ by 4-inch strips.

4. Roll almond paste into 3½-inch-long rolls 1 inch in diameter. Place each almond roll in center of dough strip. Moisten edges of dough. Enclose almond rolls; seal side and ends. Place seam side down. Shape each into desired letter.

5. Place on lightly greased baking sheet. Brush with egg glaze. Bake in a preheated 375°F oven 25 to 35 minutes, or until golden brown. Cool on a wire rack.

Dutch Saint Nicholas Fudge

This superb fudge is a tradition in Holland on Saint Nicholas' Eve. The Dutch often serve it in shapes such as hearts, stars, squares, or coins and in various flavors. *Yields 45 1 × 1-inch pieces*

> 1 *cup half-and-half*
> 1¼ *cups granulated sugar*
> 1 *cup light brown sugar, firmly packed*
> ⅛ *teaspoon salt*
> ½ *teaspoon cream of tartar*
> 2 *tablespoons cocoa*
> *walnuts (optional)*
>
> *candy thermometer; 9 × 5-inch loaf pan*

1. In a saucepan, scald half-and-half. Remove from heat. Add rest of ingredients except nuts. Stir constantly until butter melts and sugar dissolves.

2. Place over moderately high heat, stirring constantly; bring to a boil. With a pastry brush, wet sides of pan above liquid to retard crystallization. Cover. Simmer about 5 minutes, until sides of saucepan are clear of sugar crystals. Add nuts if desired.

3. Remove cover and cook over a moderate heat without stirring until temperature reaches 234°F, or until a small amount dropped into cold water forms a soft ball.

4. Remove from heat. Using a wooden spoon, beat 15 to 20 minutes, until fudge cools and thickens. Place a sheet of wax paper in the bottom of loaf pan. Grease paper. Pour fudge into pan.

24

HANUKKAH—
FESTIVAL OF LIGHTS

Hanukkah, the Festival of Lights, is a time of rejoicing among Jews. During the eight days of the holiday, Jews reflect on their history, exchange gifts, and make donations to the poor. On each of the eight days, they light an additional candle until their nine-place menorah, or candelabrum, is completely lighted (the extra candle is the one used to light the rest). This festival usually falls in December.

In Hebrew, Hanukkah means "dedication." This refers to the resolution of one of the great crises in the history of Judaism. In 167 B.C. the Syrian king Antiochus seized and defiled the Temple of Jerusalem. He looted its rich furnishings, profaned it with the sacrifice of pigs, and raised pagan statues in its holy precincts. A family called the Maccabees began guerrilla warfare against the Syrians. After three years of fighting the Maccabean warriors triumphed. They recaptured the Temple and cleansed it of pagan contamination. Then, according to the Talmud, the Maccabees were taken aback to find that they had only a day's supply of the special oil used to light the Temple menorah. To their delight, however, this oil miraculously burned for eight days.

In memory of this event, the head of a Jewish household now lights a candle each day of the holiday, from right to left, until the entire menorah is aglow. During this ceremony the entire family joins in prayer. Hanukkah is frequently also a community festival in which Jews hold parties to raise money for charity.

Bimuelos—Hanukkah Fritters

These fritters are a classic Hanukkah treat. Drizzled with honey syrup and served hot, they evoke happy holiday memories in countless Jewish households. *Yields about 4 dozen*

> 1 tablespoon active dry yeast
> ½ teaspoon granulated sugar
> 1½ cups warm water (105–115°F)
> 2½–3 cups all-purpose flour
> ⅛ teaspoon salt
> 1 egg
> vegetable oil for deep frying

> **Syrup**
> 1¼ cups honey
> 2 tablespoons lemon juice

> deep fryer

1. Dissolve yeast and sugar in ½ cup of warm water. Set aside for 5 minutes.

2. In a mixing bowl, combine 2 cups of flour, salt, remaining water, and dissolved yeast. Mix. Add egg and enough remaining flour to make a soft dough.

3. Knead on a lightly floured surface until smooth, 5 to 10 minutes. Place in a greased bowl, turning to coat top. Cover. Let rise in a warm place until double, about 45 minutes.

4. Heat oil to 375°F. Using a teaspoon dipped into cold water each time, drop small portions of batter into oil. Fry only a few fritters at a time until golden brown. Drain on paper towels.

5. To make syrup: In a small saucepan, boil honey with lemon juice 3 minutes. Place fritters on a serving platter. Pour hot honey over them. Serve at once.

Sufganiot—Israeli Jelly Doughnuts

(soof-GAHN-ee-ote)

These scrumptious doughnuts are a modern Israeli version of a traditional Hanukkah fried dessert. See how light and tasty they are! *Yields 24*

> 2 *tablespoons active dry yeast*
> ⅓ *cup granulated sugar*
> 1 *cup warm milk (105–115°F)*
> 2–2¼ *cups all-purpose flour*
> 2 *tablespoons margarine*
> 2 *egg yolks*
> ⅛ *teaspoon salt*
> ½ *tablespoon ground cinnamon*
> *vegetable oil for deep frying*
> *strawberry preserves or your choice of jam, jelly, or preserves*
> *confectioners' sugar for sprinkling on top*
>
> *deep fryer; 2-inch round cookie cutter*

1. Dissolve yeast and 1 teaspoon of sugar in ¼ cup of milk. Set aside for 5 minutes.
2. In a mixing bowl, combine 1½ cups of flour, margarine, egg yolks, salt, cinnamon, remaining sugar and milk, and dissolved yeast. Add enough remaining flour to make a soft dough.
3. Knead on a lightly floured surface until smooth, 5 to 10 minutes. Place in a greased bowl, turning to coat top. Cover. Let rise in a warm place until double, about 1 hour.
4. Punch down dough. On a lightly floured surface, roll out dough to about ½ inch thick. Using cookie cutter, cut out rounds. Cover. Let rise another 15 minutes.
5. While rounds are rising, preheat oil to 375°F. Drop only a few rounds at a time in oil. Turn when brown. Drain on paper towels. Using a small spoon, fill doughnuts with preserves.
6. Sprinkle with confectioners' sugar.

Rugelach—Cream Cheese Pastries

(roo-guh-LAKH)

These pastries are one of the classic cream cheese desserts traditional on Hanukkah. Try them with strawberry jam or raisin-nut filling. *Yields 30*

> 2 *sticks butter*
> 8 *ounces cream cheese*
> 2½ *cups all-purpose flour*
>
> **Strawberry Jam Filling** *(Try another jam if you wish.)*
> ¾ *cup finely ground almonds*
> ¾ *cup strawberry jam*
> *granulated sugar for sprinkling on top (optional)*
>
> **Raisin-Nut Filling**
> ¼ *cup granulated sugar*
> ¼ *cup dark raisins*
> 1 *teaspoon ground cinnamon*
> ½ *cup finely chopped walnuts*
> *granulated sugar for sprinkling on top (optional)*
>
> *baking sheet*

1. In a mixing bowl, cream butter and cream cheese together. Gradually add flour. Mix thoroughly. *Chill overnight.*
2. For strawberry jam filling: In a mixing bowl, combine almonds and jam. Set aside.
3. For raisin-nut filling: In a mixing bowl, combine ¼ cup of sugar, raisins, cinnamon, and walnuts. Set aside.
4. On a lightly floured surface, roll out ¼ of dough to ⅛-inch thickness. Make triangles 4 inches at the base and 6 inches high. If dough is sticky, sprinkle lightly with flour.
5. Spread about 1 teaspoon of filling over bottom half of each

triangle. Beginning with bottom, roll up triangle tightly. Place on ungreased baking sheet. If desired, sprinkle lightly with sugar.

6. Bake in a preheated 350°F oven 20 to 25 minutes, or until golden brown. Cool on baking sheet 5 minutes; then cool on a wire rack.

25

SAINT LUCIA'S DAY

DECEMBER 13

Although based on dubious evidence, Saint Lucia's Day is one of the most charming in the calendar. In Sweden and in Sicily (her birthplace), the saint and her beautiful legend are treated with special reverence. In this country, people of Swedish and Sicilian heritage, along with many others, frequently honor the traditions that surround Lucia.

According to report, Lucia vowed as a child to become a dedicated Christian. Later she was betrothed to a man whom she rejected. Her fiancé retaliated by informing pagan authorities that Lucia was a Christian. She survived horrible tortures rather than forswear her faith before finally being dispatched by a sword in the year 304.

In Syracuse, Italy, a silver statue of Saint Lucia and her bier are put on display in the cathedral on December 5. Then, on December 13, the bier is ceremoniously carried down illuminated streets past houses hung with colorful cloths.

Saint Lucia's Day officially starts the Christmas season in Sweden. Early in the morning, the daughter of a household dresses up in a white dress, red sash, and red stockings. On her head is an evergreen crown with five candles set in it. Bearing a tray holding coffee and yellow buns called Saint Lucia's Cats (for recipe, see *The Festive Bread Book*), she sings a song at each bedroom door to awaken the sleepers. Then she serves each with coffee and the cats.

Other delicacies too have become traditional on Saint Lucia's Day, such as the one that follows.

Luciapepparkakor—Saint Lucia Gingersnaps

(lu-chee-a-PEP-er-kak-er)

The girl carrying out the role of Saint Lucia often offers these tangy gingersnaps to members of the family and guests early in the morning. *Yields about 4 dozen*

> 1 *cup heavy cream*
> 1¼ *cups light brown sugar, firmly packed*
> ⅓ *cup dark molasses*
> ⅓ *cup dark corn syrup*
> ½ *tablespoon ground ginger*
> ½ *tablespoon grated lemon rind*
> ½ *tablespoon baking soda*
> ¼ *teaspoon ground cloves*
> ½ *teaspoon ground cinnamon*
> 4 *cups all-purpose flour*
>
> **Confectioners' Icing** *(optional)*
> 1 *cup confectioners' sugar*
> 1–2 *tablespoons water*
> ½ *teaspoon almond extract*
>
> *cookie cutters; baking sheet*

1. In a mixing bowl, beat cream until slightly stiff. Add sugar, molasses, corn syrup, ginger, lemon rind, baking soda, cloves, and cinnamon. Mix thoroughly.

2. Gradually add flour, about ½ cup at a time. Mix thoroughly after each addition. Cover bowl; chill overnight.

3. On a lightly floured board, roll out dough to ⅛-inch thickness. (Keep dough chilled when not in use.) Use desired cookie cutters. Place on lightly greased baking sheet.

4. Bake in a preheated 325°F oven about 10 to 15 minutes, or until light brown. Cool on wire rack.

5. If desired, make icing: Mix sugar, water, and almond extract. Decorate.

26

CHRISTMAS

DECEMBER 25

The birth of Christ is celebrated the world over in a profusion of customs hallowed by time. At heart, of course, the Christmas story is simple. The Christ Child is born in a manger because his parents can find no room to stay in Bethlehem, where they have gone to pay their taxes. There, nestled amid straw, the Christ Child is visited by divinely inspired shepherds from "the same country" and by wise men, or Magi (the Bible doesn't say how many), from distant lands.

Until the fourth century, the day of Christ's birth was not regarded as a holiday. Christians paid much more attention to other key points in His life, such as His Passion and Crucifixion. But around the year 350 we begin to hear of Christmas celebrations, with the Church of Rome making December 25 officially the Feast of the Nativity.

Christmas falls at a time of year steeped in ancient religious lore. December 25 almost coincides with the solstice, that time in the Northern Hemisphere when the winter sun seems to be rising after having sunk to its lowest point. Followers of many early faiths greeted this event with relief and thanksgiving.

Two Roman festivals reflecting pagan traditions especially helped shape the Christmas celebration. The Romans celebrated Saturnalia, a week-long holiday beginning December 17, with public decorations and unbridled merriment. They then celebrated Kalends, a three-day holiday beginning January 1, with gift-giving and parties at which masters and servants mingled in a spirit of fellowship.

Northern European peoples contributed distinctive customs of their own. The Celts celebrated their new year from November into January. At raucous parties they feasted on cattle slaughtered because the animals would be unable to survive bitter winter weather. Ale and mead helped revelers forget the long and dreary time they would endure before the beginning of spring.

Another European custom that became widely popular was the Yule log. This was a tree trunk dragged into the house with ceremony. People traditionally lighted it with pieces from the preceding year's Yule log. The log was partially burned on each of the twelve days of the Christmas season and surviving fragments were preserved for the following year.

The origin of Christmas greens and the Christmas tree is less clear than some other Christian customs, but European pagans did worship in sacred groves. According to some authorities, Martin Luther introduced the idea of an indoor Christmas tree and lighted his tree with candles symbolizing stars. Subsequently, German emigrants carried the tradition of a Christmas tree with them, persuading their neighbors by example to adopt the custom.

Religious reform took a heavy toll on Christmas traditions. Early citizens of New England, regarding the customs surrounding it as merely pagan, did not observe Christmas as a holiday. In the Massachusetts Bay Colony, taking the day off or otherwise observing Christmas was punishable by a fine of five shillings. Even at the beginning of the nineteenth century, Christmas was still not a federal holiday, nor did states give it legal recognition. It took the moderating influence of time and the strong Christmas traditions of various immigrant groups to establish Christmas ceremony in the United States not only as an occasion of merriment, but also as an affirmation of the yearning for peace and goodwill on earth.

Feasting has usually been a central part of the traditional Christmas celebration. And it is on this occasion that one finds the greatest and most delectable variety of holiday desserts. You will find here a dazzling array of special cakes, cookies, puddings, pies, and candies celebrating what many feel is the happiest day of the year.

Coconut Snowball Cake

Coconuts were often associated with Christmas in the Southern United States because they became available in December. This white cake, beautifully covered with coconut frosting, is a Christmas favorite in many Southern localities. You will find the cake rich and satisfying but not at all cloying. *Yields 1 cake*

> 2½ cups all-purpose flour
> 1½ tablespoons baking powder
> ½ teaspoon salt
> 1 tablespoon grated lemon peel
> 1½ sticks butter
> 1½ cups granulated sugar
> ¼ cup lemon juice
> ⅔ cup milk
> ½ teaspoon lemon extract
> 6 egg whites, beaten stiff
>
> **Frosting**
> 2 egg whites
> 1 cup granulated sugar
> ½ teaspoon cream of tartar
> ⅓ cup boiling water
> ⅛ teaspoon salt
> 1 teaspoon lemon extract
> grated fresh coconut or, *if preferred, canned coconut*
>
> 2 9-inch round cake pans

1. In a small bowl, combine flour, baking powder, salt, and lemon peel. Set aside. In a mixing bowl, cream butter and sugar until light and fluffy.

2. Mix lemon juice with milk. Add this milk to creamed butter alternately with flour mixture. Stir in lemon extract. Fold in egg whites.

3. Grease pans. Lightly dust with flour. Pour ½ of batter in each prepared pan. Bake in a preheated 350°F oven 25 to 30 minutes, or until a cake tester comes out clean. Cool in pan 10 minutes. Remove cake from pan and cool on a wire rack 10 minutes.

4. In a small bowl, combine all frosting ingredients except lemon extract. Beat at high speed 10 minutes, or until stiff peaks stand up. Fold in lemon extract.

5. Place 1 layer of cake upside down on a serving plate. Spread thick layer of frosting on the top. Sprinkle coconut thickly on frosting. Place second layer of cake on top of frosting. Cover top and sides of cake with frosting. Sprinkle thickly with coconut. Refrigerate.

Shaker Christmas Cake

Shaker Christmas celebrations differed from one Shaker village to another. Some prepared for the holiday weeks in advance, composing new hymns, sewing articles of clothing, and assembling the ingredients of Christmas foods. This cake with a maple syrup frosting was a specialty in the North Union Shaker Village in Ohio. *Yields 1 cake*

> 3¼ cups all-purpose flour
> 1 tablespoon baking powder
> ½ teaspoon salt
> 1 cup granulated sugar
> 2 sticks butter
> 1 cup milk
> ½ tablespoon rosewater
> 6 egg whites
> ¾ cup chopped pecans

Maple Syrup Icing
3/4 cup maple syrup
2 egg whites
1/4 teaspoon salt
1/2 teaspoon cream of tartar

chopped pecans for top and sides of cake

2 8-inch cake pans; candy thermometer

1. In a bowl, combine flour, baking powder, and salt. Set aside. In a mixing bowl, cream sugar and butter until light and fluffy.

2. Gradually add flour mixture and milk alternately. Stir in rosewater. Beat egg whites until stiff peaks stand up. Fold into cake batter. Stir in nuts.

3. Pour batter into greased and floured cake pans. Bake in a preheated 350°F oven 30 to 40 minutes, or until a cake tester comes out clean. Cool on a wire rack.

4. To make icing: Boil maple syrup until candy thermometer reads 230°F. In a bowl, combine egg whites, salt, and cream of tartar until stiff peaks stand up. Very slowly add heated maple syrup to egg white mixture. Beat until frosting is thick enough to spread.

5. Ice cake and sprinkle nuts on top and sides.

Grischdagringel—
Pennsylvania Dutch Christmas Ring

Topped with whipped cream, this ultra-rich fruitcake is almost a Christmas feast in itself. *Yields 1 cake*

3/4 cup chopped dates
3/4 cup chopped walnuts
1/2 cup all-purpose flour

²/₃ *cup light brown sugar, firmly packed*
½ *tablespoon baking powder*
2 *eggs, separated*
1 *teaspoon vanilla extract*
¼ *cup sweet sherry*
⅛ *teaspoon salt*

Topping
1 *cup heavy cream*
3 *tablespoons confectioners' sugar*
1 *teaspoon vanilla extract*
candied citron
candied orange peel
maraschino cherries

8-inch ring pan

1. In a small bowl, combine dates, walnuts, and 1 tablespoon of the flour. Toss.

2. In a mixing bowl, combine remaining flour, brown sugar, baking powder, egg yolks, vanilla, sherry, and salt. Mix thoroughly. Add date-and-nut mixture. Mix.

3. Beat egg whites until stiff peaks stand up. Fold egg whites into mixture.

4. Pour into greased and floured pan. Bake in a preheated 350°F oven 30 minutes, or until a cake tester comes out clean. Cool in pan. Remove cake from mold and place on a serving plate.

5. Whip cream until stiff. Fold in sugar. Stir in vanilla. Spread on top of ring. On whipped cream, make a wreath with citron and orange peel leaves and cherry berries. (Use your imagination!)

Pastel de Noche Buena— Mexican Christmas Eve Cake

(pahs-TEL day NO-chay BWAY-na)

This rich spicy cake is a beloved delicacy eaten on Christmas Eve in Mexico. *Yields 1 cake*

> 1/3 *cup candied lemon peel*
> 1/3 *cup candied orange peel*
> 1/3 *cup candied citron peel*
> 1/2 *cup currants*
> 1/2 *cup dark raisins*
> 1/3 *cup brandy*
> 1   *cup granulated sugar*
> 1   *pound butter*
> 8   *eggs*
> 1   *tablespoon ground cinnamon*
> 1/2 *tablespoon ground mace*
> 1   *teaspoon ground cloves*
> 1   *teaspoon ground nutmeg*
> 1/2 *tablespoon baking powder*
> 1/2 *teaspoon salt*
> 3 3/4 *cups flour*
>
> *12-cup Bundt pan*

1. In a bowl, combine fruit peels, currants, raisins, and brandy. Mix and leave on counter overnight.

2. In a mixing bowl, cream sugar and butter until light and fluffy. Add eggs 1 at a time, beating after each addition. Add spices, baking powder, salt, and 3 cups of the flour.

3. Drain the fruit and pour the brandy into batter. Add remaining flour to the fruit. Stir into batter.

4. Pour batter into greased Bundt pan. Bake in a preheated 300°F oven 2 to 2½ hours, or until a cake tester comes out clean. Cool on a wire rack.

Dundee Cake

This fruitcake, originating in Scotland, offers a full-flavored conclusion to a Christmas meal. It can also be an enjoyable and filling holiday snack. *Yields 1 cake*

> 2 *sticks butter*
> ¾ *cup granulated sugar*
> 3 *eggs*
> 2½ *cups all-purpose flour*
> 1 *teaspoon baking powder*
> ¼ *teaspoon salt*
> 1 *tablespoon grated orange peel*
> ½ *tablespoon grated lemon peel*
> ½ *cup milk*
> ⅓ *cup currants*
> ½ *cup golden raisins*
> ⅓ *cup chopped mixed candied fruit peel*
> ½ *cup chopped blanched almonds*
> *blanched whole almonds*
>
> *8-inch springform pan*

1. Grease pan with butter. Lightly dust flour on bottom and sides.

2. In a mixing bowl, cream butter and sugar until light and fluffy. Add eggs 1 at a time, beating after each addition.

3. In a small bowl, combine flour, baking powder, salt, and orange and lemon peels. Mix. Gradually add flour mixture and milk to batter. Mix.

4. Fold in remaining ingredients except whole almonds. Make an arrangement of whole almonds on bottom of greased pan. (Use your imagination here!) Pour in batter.

5. Bake in a preheated 350°F oven 1¼ hours, or until a cake tester comes out clean. Cool cake in pan 10 minutes; then cool on a wire rack. Wrap in foil and refrigerate.

Plum Cake

In this magnificent fruitcake, a Christmas tradition from the days
of Olde England, the "plums" are actually raisins. *Yields 1 cake*

> 3 cups all-purpose flour
> 1/2 cup currants
> 1/2 cup dark raisins
> 1/2 cup golden raisins
> 1/2 cup cherries
> 1/2 cup chopped candied lemon peel
> 1/2 cup chopped candied orange peel
> 2 sticks butter
> 1/3 cup light brown sugar, firmly packed
> 5 eggs
> 3 tablespoons lemon juice
> 1 tablespoon grated lemon rind
> 1 teaspoon ground cinnamon
> 1/2 teaspoon ground cloves
> 1/2 teaspoon ground nutmeg
> 1/2 teaspoon ground allspice
> 1 teaspoon baking soda
> 1/2 cup dark molasses
> 1/2 cup chopped blanched almonds
> 2/3 cup chopped walnuts
> 1/4 cup apple cider
> 1/2 cup brandy
>
> 10-inch tube pan

1. In a mixing bowl, combine 1/4 cup of the flour, currants,
dark and golden raisins, cherries, and lemon and orange peels.
Mix. Set aside.

2. In a mixing bowl, cream butter and sugar until light and
fluffy. Add eggs 1 at a time, beating after each addition. Add
lemon juice and rind, spices, baking soda, and molasses. Mix.

3. Add remaining flour, nuts, and fruit mixture. Mix. Add apple cider and brandy. Mix well.

4. Pour batter into greased pan. Bake in a preheated 350°F oven about 60 minutes, or until a cake tester comes out clean. Cool in pan 10 minutes. Remove and cool on a wire rack.

Irish Christmas Fruitcake

Here's a white fruitcake greatly admired in Irish households. Plump with candied cherries, raisins, and currants, it richly completes a Christmas meal. *Yields 1 cake*

> ⅔ *cup chopped candied cherries*
> 1 *cup dark raisins*
> 1 *cup golden raisins*
> 1 *cup currants*
> ¾ *cup chopped mixed candied fruit peel*
> 2 *cups all-purpose flour*
> 2 *sticks butter*
> 1 *cup granulated sugar*
> 5 *eggs*
> 1 *teaspoon ground allspice*
> ½ *teaspoon salt*
> ½ *teaspoon baking soda*

> *10-inch Bundt pan*

1. In a small bowl, combine cherries, raisins, currants, fruit peel, and ¼ cup of the flour. Set aside.

2. In a mixing bowl, cream butter and sugar until light and fluffy. Add eggs 1 at a time, beating after each addition.

3. In a small bowl, combine remaining flour, allspice, salt, and baking soda. Gradually add dry ingredients and fruit mixture.

4. Pour into greased and lightly floured pan. Bake in a preheated 350°F oven about 2 hours, or until a cake tester comes out clean. Cool on a wire rack.

Bûche de Noël—French Yule Log

(BOOSH de no-EL)

This spectacular cake, shaped and decorated to look like a Yule log, is a classic Christmas dessert in France. It is rich and just as scrumptious as it looks. *Yields 1 cake*

> 1 cup all-purpose flour
> 1 teaspoon baking powder
> ¼ teaspoon salt
> ¼ cup unsweetened cocoa
> 5 eggs
> ¾ cup confectioners' sugar
> 1 teaspoon vanilla extract
> confectioners' sugar for coating

Filling

> 1 cup heavy cream, chilled
> ⅓ cup confectioners' sugar
> ¼ cup unsweetened cocoa
> 1 teaspoon instant coffee
> ½ teaspoon vanilla extract

Icing

> 1½ sticks butter
> 1 pound sifted confectioners' sugar
> ¼ cup unsweetened cocoa
> 3–4 tablespoons brandy
> candied cherries (optional)
> candied citron (optional)
> finely chopped pistachio nuts (optional)

> 15½ × 10½ × 1-inch jelly-roll pan

1. Grease pan. Line pan with wax paper; grease paper and sprinkle lightly with flour. (Remove any excess flour from pan.)

2. In a bowl, combine flour, baking powder, salt, and cocoa. Set aside. In a mixing bowl, beat eggs until light and fluffy. Gradually add sugar and vanilla. Mix.

3. Gradually add dry ingredients. Mix thoroughly. Fold batter into prepared pan. Bake in a preheated 400°F oven 12 to 15 minutes, or until a cake tester comes out clean.

4. While cake is baking, sprinkle confectioners' sugar on a towel. When the cake is baked, invert cake on the towel. Peel wax paper off the cake. Trim off any crusty edges.

5. Gently roll up cake, starting with long edge, including towel. Unroll; remove towel; roll up again. Cool, seam side down.

6. While cake is cooling, make filling. Beat cream until slightly thickened. Add sugar, cocoa, coffee, and vanilla. Beat until thoroughly mixed. Cover in refrigerator until ready to use.

7. Unroll cake gently. Spread with filling, leaving 1-inch margin all the way around. Reroll as tightly as possible.

8. With seam side down, put on a serving plate. If desired, slice 1 inch off end of cake to serve as a knot.

9. To make frosting: Combine butter, sugar, cocoa, and brandy. Frost rim of the "knot" and place it on the side or top of cake. Frost cake, using the tines of a fork to score surface for a barklike effect.

10. Decorate with "holly" made from candied cherries and candied citron strips. If desired, cover the ends of the cake with finely chopped pistachio nuts.

NOTES: If preferred, use plastic holly leaves for decoration instead of citron.

May be stored up to a week in the refrigerator.

Decorate with meringue mushrooms (see page 239).

Bûche aux Marrons—French Chestnut Yule Log

(BOOSH oh ma-ROHN)

Similar to Bûche de Noël (preceding recipe), this cake is distinguished by a filling fabulously flavored with puréed chestnuts. *Yields 1 cake*

> 1 cup all-purpose flour
> 1 teaspoon baking powder
> ¼ cup cocoa
> 5 eggs
> ⅔ cup confectioners' sugar
> 1 teaspoon vanilla extract
> confectioners' sugar for coating

Filling
> 1 stick butter
> ⅔ cup confectioners' sugar
> 1-pound can sweetened chestnuts, puréed
> ¼ cup kirsch
> crystallized violets (optional)

> 15½ × 10½ × 1-inch jelly-roll pan

1. Grease pan. Line pan with wax paper; grease paper and sprinkle lightly with flour. (Remove any excess flour from pan.)

2. In a bowl, combine flour, baking powder, and cocoa. Set aside. In a mixing bowl, beat eggs until light and fluffy. Gradually add sugar and vanilla. Mix.

3. Gradually add dry ingredients. Mix thoroughly. Fold batter into prepared pan. Bake in a preheated 400°F oven 12 to 15 minutes, or until a cake tester comes out clean.

4. While cake is baking, sprinkle confectioners' sugar on a towel. When the cake is baked, invert cake on the towel. Peel wax paper off the cake. Trim off any crusty edges.

5. Gently roll up cake, starting with long edge, including towel. Unroll; remove towel; roll up again. Cool, seam side down.

6. While cake is cooling, make filling: Cream butter and sugar together until light and fluffy. Add chestnuts and kirsch.

7. Unroll cake gently. Spread ½ of filling, leaving 1-inch margin all the way around. Reroll as tightly as possible.

8. With seam side down, put on a serving plate. If desired, slice 1 inch off end of cake to serve as a knot.

9. Frost with remaining filling. Using the tines of a fork, score surface for a barklike effect. Decorate with candied violets if desired.

NOTE: May be stored in refrigerator a day or two.

Cucidata—Italian Fig Cake

(KOO-chee-DAH-ta)

A delicious fig-and-nut filling inside a buttery crust makes this a traditional Italian Christmas treat. *Yields 3 cakes*

> 4 *cups all-purpose flour*
> ½ *tablespoon baking powder*
> ½ *teaspoon salt*
> ¾ *cup granulated sugar*
> 1 *tablespoon grated lemon rind*
> ⅔ *cup lard*
> 2 *sticks butter*
> ¼ *cup brandy*
> ¼–½ *cup ice water*

Filling

1½ cups dark raisins
14-ounce package dried figs
1¼ cups blanched toasted almonds
¾ cup chopped walnuts
1 tablespoon grated lemon rind
1 tablespoon grated orange rind
1 teaspoon ground cinnamon
¼ cup orange juice
confectioners' sugar for sprinkling on top

baking sheet

1. In a mixing bowl, combine flour, baking powder, salt, sugar, and lemon rind. Cut in lard and butter with two knives or a pastry blender until mixture resembles fine meal.

2. Add brandy and enough water to make medium-soft and manageable. Knead 3 to 4 minutes. Then place in a bowl and refrigerate 1 hour.

3. To make filling: Combine raisins, figs, and nuts. Put through a food grinder, using a coarse blade. Place in a mixing bowl. Add fruit rinds, cinnamon, and orange juice. Mix and set aside until ready to use.

4. Divide dough into thirds and roll each third out to ⅛-inch thickness, 4 inches wide and 16 inches long.

5. Place filling 1 inch wide in center of each strip. Fold dough over filling. Pinch edges together. Shape resulting tubes into rings. Using a sharp knife, make diagonal slashes every inch around each ring.

6. Place on greased baking sheet. Bake in a preheated 375°F oven 20 to 25 minutes, or until golden brown. Cool on a wire rack. Sprinkle with confectioners' sugar before serving.

Flaeskekage—Danish Pork Cake

(FLES-ke-KAY-ya)

This hearty fruitcake makes a good change of pace from lighter Christmas cakes. The Danes prize pork cake as more than just a dessert—it's a treat that sticks to a person's ribs at a time of inclement weather and strenuous activity. *Yields 1 cake*

> 4½ cups all-purpose flour
> 1 teaspoon ground cinnamon
> ½ teaspoon ground cloves
> ½ teaspoon ground nutmeg
> ½ teaspoon ground allspice
> 1 pound salt pork
> 2 cups boiling water
> ⅔ cup dark molasses
> 1¾ cups brown sugar, firmly packed
> ½ tablespoon baking soda
> ½ cup chopped citron
> ½ cup chopped candied cherries
> 1 cup chopped dates
> 1 cup golden raisins
>
> 12-cup Bundt pan

1. In a bowl, combine flour and spices.
2. Grind pork in a food processor or chop finely by hand. Pour in boiling water. Add molasses, sugar, and baking soda. Mix.
3. Stir in citron, candied cherries, dates, and raisins. Gradually add flour mixture. Mix thoroughly.
4. Pour batter into greased and lightly floured Bundt pan. Place in a preheated 350°F oven 1¼ to 1½ hours, or until a cake tester comes out clean. Cool on a wire rack.

NOTE: May be kept indefinitely in a refrigerator or freezer.

Brun Julekage—Danish Fruitcake

(BROON YUL-e-KAY-ya)

One of the most delectable Christmas fruitcakes, laden with candied fruit and spirits, this Danish tradition deserves to be much more widely enjoyed. *Yields 1 cake*

> 1 *cup dark raisins*
> 1 *cup currants*
> 1/2 *cup candied orange peel*
> 1/2 *cup candied lemon peel*
> 1/2 *cup candied pineapple*
> 1/2 *cup candied cherries*
> 1/2 *cup red wine*
> 1/2 *cup brandy*
> 1 *cup granulated sugar*
> 2 *sticks butter*
> 2/3 *cup dark molasses*
> 10 *eggs*
> 5 1/2 *cups flour*
> 1/2 *tablespoon baking powder*
> 1/2 *tablespoon ground cinnamon*
> 1 *teaspoon ground allspice*
> 1 *teaspoon ground nutmeg*
> 1 *cup light cream*
> 1 *cup blanched almonds, coarsely chopped*
> *brandy or wine for soaking*
>
> *10-inch Bundt pan; cheesecloth*

1. In a mixing bowl, combine raisins, currants, fruit peels, pineapple, cherries, wine, and brandy. Mix. Set aside overnight.

2. In another mixing bowl, cream sugar and butter until light and fluffy. Add molasses. Add eggs 1 at a time, beating after each addition.

3. In a third mixing bowl, combine 5 cups of the flour, baking powder, and spices. Gradually add to batter. Add cream.

4. Drain fruit. Add liquid from fruit to batter. Add remaining flour to fruit. Toss. Add fruit to batter.

5. Add almonds and mix. Pour batter into greased Bundt pan. Bake in a preheated 275°F oven about 4 hours, or until a cake tester comes out clean.

6. Cool on a wire rack. Wrap in cheesecloth. Soak in brandy or wine. Dampen cheesecloth whenever necessary.

NOTE: Make 2 weeks to 2 months before serving.

Pepparkakshus—Swedish Gingerbread House

(PEP-er-koks-hoos)

Gingerbread houses are a highlight of Christmas in many countries. The young especially love helping to make—and eat—them. The following recipe is from Sweden, where children customarily create the house with their mothers' guidance. *Yields 1 house, plus gingerbread men, Christmas tree, etc.*

> 1⅓ *cups dark brown sugar, firmly packed*
> 1⅓ *cups dark corn syrup*
> 2 *sticks butter*
> ½ *tablespoon baking soda*
> ¾ *cup heavy cream*
> 1 *tablespoon ground cinnamon*
> 1 *tablespoon ground ginger*
> 8 *cups all-purpose flour*

> **Icing**
> 1¾ *cups confectioners' sugar*
> 1 *egg white*
> 1 *teaspoon lemon juice*

candy for roof (optional)
grated coconut (optional)
(If you decorate the house exclusively with icing rather than with candy, you may need to make more icing.)

baking sheets; pastry bag and writing tube; sheets of stiff cardboard covered with foil or the like.

1. In a saucepan, heat brown sugar, corn syrup, and butter over medium heat. Stir frequently until blended. Allow to cool. Dissolve baking soda in cream.

2. In a mixing bowl, combine brown sugar mixture, cream mixture, cinnamon, ginger, and flour. Mix thoroughly. Knead until smooth. Shape into a ball. Wrap airtight and place in a covered bowl. Refrigerate overnight.

3. On a lightly floured surface, roll out dough to ¼-inch thickness. Before cutting, place on greased baking sheet.

Roofs: Cut out two 9 by 4½-inch rectangles.

Front and back: Cut out two 8 by 4½-inch rectangles. As desired, cut doorway and small rectangular windows. If desired, halve the pieces removed to make windows and use for shutters. Keep piece removed for doorway and use for open door.

Ends of house: Cut out two pieces like this:

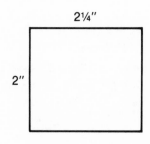

2¼"

2"

Chimney: Cut out two pieces like this:

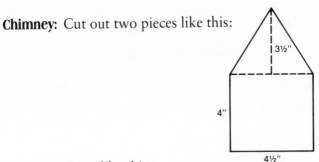

Cut out two pieces like this:

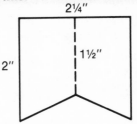

Other pieces: Cut out gingerbread man and gingerbread woman, animals, Christmas tree, etc.

4. Bake in a preheated 375°F oven 12 to 15 minutes for larger pieces, 6 to 8 minutes for smaller pieces, or until dough is firm. Let pieces cool on baking sheet.

5. For icing: In a mixing bowl, combine confectioners' sugar, egg white, and lemon juice. Beat until stiff enough to pass through pastry bag.

6. Assemble on board, using icing to join parts. Join ends and walls together. Let dry a few hours. Put on roof and chimney. Let dry. Attach shutters, door, and any other accessories.

7. Decorate house. Put candies on as shingles, or ice the roof. To make snow, sprinkle grated coconut over frosting. Place mirror as pond. Use your imagination in decorating the house and its grounds!

Melachrino—Greek Spice Cake

(meh-la-kree-NOH)

This fragrant cake, a tradition in Greece, makes a perfect Christmas treat. *Yields 1 cake*

> 1⅔ cups all-purpose flour
> 1 teaspoon ground cinnamon
> ½ teaspoon ground mace
> ½ teaspoon ground cloves
> 1 teaspoon baking soda
> ½ teaspoon salt
> 1½ sticks butter
> 1½ cups granulated sugar
> 3 eggs
> ⅔ cup milk
> 1 tablespoon lemon juice

> **Icing**
> 1½ cups confectioners' sugar
> 4–6 tablespoons water
> 1 tablespoon lemon juice

> 8-inch square cake pan

1. In a bowl, combine flour, spices, baking soda, and salt. Toss and set aside.
2. In a mixing bowl, cream butter and sugar until light and fluffy. Add eggs 1 at a time, beating after each addition.
3. Alternately add milk and flour mixture to batter. Stir in lemon juice. Grease and flour cake pan. Pour batter into pan. Bake in a preheated 350°F oven 30 to 35 minutes, or until a cake tester comes out clean.
4. While cake is baking, make icing: Combine sugar, water, and lemon juice. Ice cake while it is warm.

Polish Christmas Bread

Tested at an office coffee klatch, this Polish quick bread disappeared as if by magic. *Yields 1 loaf*

> ½ *cup finely chopped walnuts*
> ⅓ *cup golden raisins*
> ⅓ *cup candied orange peel, finely chopped*
> 2½ *cups all-purpose flour*
> 2¼ *cups confectioners' sugar*
> 2 *sticks butter*
> 3 *eggs*
> 2 *tablespoons vodka*
> 1 *tablespoon grated lemon rind*
> ½ *tablespoon baking powder*
> *bread crumbs for sprinkling in pan*
> *confectioners' sugar for sprinkling on top (optional)*
>
> 9 × 5 × 3-inch loaf pan

1. In a bowl, combine walnuts, raisins, and orange peel. Dust with 2 tablespoons of the flour. Set aside.

2. In a mixing bowl, beat sugar and butter until light and fluffy. Add eggs 1 at a time, beating after each addition.

3. Add vodka, lemon rind, baking powder, and remaining flour. Mix. Fold in fruit-nut mixture. Grease pan. Lightly sprinkle sides and bottom of pan with bread crumbs. Pour batter into pan.

4. Bake in a preheated 300°F oven 2 hours, or until a cake tester comes out clean. Cool in pan 10 minutes. Remove and cool on a wire rack.

NOTE: For best flavor, allow to mellow 1 or 2 days.

If desired, sprinkle with confectioners' sugar before serving.

Light Christmas Cake from Warsaw

This fruitcake, a tradition in Poland, is lighter than many fruit-cakes, but with a spicy flavor that rivals any. *Yields 1 cake*

> 3¼ cups all-purpose flour
> ⅔ cup candied orange peel, finely chopped
> ⅔ cup golden raisins
> ⅔ cup dried figs, coarsely chopped
> ⅔ cup pitted dried prunes, coarsely chopped
> 1¾ cups confectioners' sugar
> 2 sticks butter
> 5 eggs
> 1 tablespoon grated lemon rind
> 1 teaspoon vanilla extract
> ⅓ cup brandy
> ½ tablespoon baking powder
> ¼ teaspoon salt
> ⅔ cup coarsely chopped walnuts

Glaze
> 1 cup confectioners' sugar
> 2 tablespoons lemon juice
> ½ tablespoon grated lemon peel

> 10-inch tube pan or Bundt pan

1. In a bowl, combine ¼ cup of the flour, orange peel, raisins, figs, and prunes. Toss and set aside.

2. In a mixing bowl, combine sugar and butter. Beat until light and fluffy. Add eggs 1 at a time, beating after each addition.

3. Add lemon rind, vanilla, brandy, remaining flour, baking powder, and salt. Fold in fruit mixture and walnuts. Place in a lightly greased pan. Bake in a preheated 350°F oven 50 to 60 minutes, or until a cake tester comes out clean. Cool in pan about 10 minutes, then on a wire rack.

4. To make lemon glaze: Combine sugar, lemon juice, and lemon peel. Mix thoroughly. Drizzle on cooled cake.

Medivnyk—Ukrainian Honey Cake

(med-iv-NIK)

This cake, one of the honey desserts for which the Ukraine is famous, is a Christmas tradition. Although rich in spices and dried fruits, Medivnyk has a delightfully mellow taste—a perfect complement to any Christmas dinner. *Yields 1 cake*

¾ *cup honey*
½ *tablespoon ground cinnamon*
½ *teaspoon ground cloves*
½ *teaspoon ground nutmeg*
½ *tablespoon baking soda*
1 *stick butter*
¾ *cup light brown sugar, firmly packed*
3 *eggs, separated*
3½ *cups all-purpose flour*
½ *teaspoon salt*
½ *tablespoon baking powder*
½ *cup golden raisins*
⅓ *cup currants*
½ *cup chopped dates*
⅔ *cup chopped walnuts*

9 × 5-inch loaf pan

1. In a saucepan, bring honey to a boil. Add spices and baking soda. Cool.

2. In a mixing bowl, cream butter and sugar until light and fluffy. Add egg yolks 1 at a time, beating after each addition. Add honey mixture. Mix thoroughly.

3. Gradually add 3¼ cups of the flour, salt, and baking powder. Mix thoroughly.

4. In a small bowl, combine raisins, currants, dates, and nuts with remaining flour. Stir into batter.

5. In a bowl, beat egg whites until stiff peaks stand up. Fold into batter.

6. Pour into greased and floured pan. Bake in a preheated 350°F oven about 1½ hours, or until a cake tester comes out clean. Cool on a wire rack.

NOTE: Store cake a few days to improve flavor.

Sooji Cake—Christmas Cake from India

This fruit-and-nut cake is a Christmas favorite among Christians in India. A custom associated with this cake is for the head of the family to put the mixed fruit into the batter, naming a member of the family as each scoopful is added. *Yields 1 cake*

> 1 *cup golden raisins*
> 2 *tablespoons crystallized ginger, coarsely chopped*
> 2 *tablespoons candied orange peel*
> 2 *tablespoons candied lemon peel*
> ½ *cup blanched almonds, coarsely chopped*
> 1 *tablespoon rosewater*
> 4 *tablespoons rum*
> ½ *tablespoon ground nutmeg*
> ½ *teaspoon ground cardamom*
> ½ *teaspoon caraway seeds*
> ½ *teaspoon ground mace*

2   *cups granulated sugar*
6   *eggs, separated*
1¼ *cups farina*
1½ *sticks butter*
¼   *cup whole wheat flour*

*large jar; soufflé pan, about 7-inch diameter
and 4-inch depth, or the equivalent;
larger pan to hold soufflé pan for steaming*

1. In a large jar, combine raisins, ginger, fruit peels, almonds, rosewater, rum, nutmeg, cardamom, caraway seeds, and mace. Mix thoroughly. Set aside about 1 week, mixing daily.

2. In a mixing bowl, combine sugar and eggs. Beat until light and fluffy. Add farina and butter. Mix thoroughly. Gradually add fruit mixture, beating constantly. Add flour. Mix.

3. Pour batter into greased soufflé pan. Cover with foil. Place soufflé pan in larger pan. Pour enough water into larger pan to reach ⅔ of the way up the sides of the soufflé pan. Steam 2 hours.

4. Remove foil and bake cake in a preheated 325°F oven 40 to 50 minutes, or until top turns brown. Cool in pan about 10 minutes. Place on a cake plate.

Moravian White Christmas Cookies

These delicate white cookies may be cut into different holiday shapes and sprinkled with colored sugar, chopped nuts, or candied fruit for a festive treat at Christmastime. *Yields 6 dozen 2-inch cookies*

> 2 *sticks butter*
> 2 *cups granulated sugar*
> 3 *eggs*
> ¼ *cup sherry*
> 4 *cups all-purpose flour*
> 1 *teaspoon ground cinnamon*
> ½ *teaspoon ground nutmeg*
>
> *2-inch cookie cutters; baking sheet*

1. In a mixing bowl, cream butter and sugar until light and fluffy. Add eggs 1 at a time, beating after each addition.
2. Add sherry. Mix thoroughly. Gradually add flour, cinnamon, and nutmeg. Mix thoroughly. Refrigerate dough overnight.
3. On a lightly floured surface, roll out dough to ⅛-inch thickness. With desired cookie cutters, cut into holiday shapes. Place on greased baking sheet.
4. Bake in a preheated 350°F oven 10 to 12 minutes, or until lightly browned. Cool on a wire rack.

NOTE: Store in an airtight container.

Moravian Dark Christmas Cookies

These cookies are much like Moravian White Christmas Cookies (preceding recipe) but with a spicier flavor. The dark cookies also may be cut into different holiday shapes and sprinkled with colored sugar, chopped nuts, or candied fruit. *Yields 7 dozen 2-inch cookies*

> 2 tablespoons butter
> ½ cup dark brown sugar, firmly packed
> ¾ cup dark molasses
> 2¾ cups all-purpose flour
> ¼ teaspoon salt
> ½ teaspoon baking soda
> ½ teaspoon ground cinnamon
> ½ teaspoon ground cloves
> ½ teaspoon ground ginger
> ¼ teaspoon ground nutmeg
> ¼ teaspoon ground allspice
>
> *2-inch cookie cutters; baking sheet*

1. In a mixing bowl, cream butter and sugar until light and fluffy. Add molasses and mix.
2. Gradually add flour, salt, baking soda, and spices. Refrigerate dough overnight.
3. On a lightly floured surface, roll out dough to ⅛-inch thickness. With desired cookie cutters, cut into holiday shapes. Place on greased baking sheet.
4. Bake in a preheated 350°F oven 8 to 10 minutes, or until even golden brown. Cool on a wire rack.

NOTE: Store in an airtight container.

Sandtarts—
Pennsylvania Dutch Christmas Cookies

These famed butter cookies from the Pennsylvania Dutch country are made in tiny tart pans. A very similar cookie is a Christmas favorite in Sweden as well. *Yields 3½ dozen*

2 *cups granulated sugar*
2 *sticks butter*
3 *eggs*
3½ *cups all-purpose flour*
½ *teaspoon salt*
½ *tablespoon baking powder*
1 *teaspoon lemon extract*

Sandbakelse molds (available in most department stores); baking sheet

1. In a mixing bowl, cream sugar and butter until light and fluffy. Add eggs 1 at a time, beating after each addition.
2. Gradually add flour, salt, baking powder, and lemon extract. Refrigerate dough ovenright.
3. In ungreased molds, press 1 or 2 teaspoonfuls of dough over bottom and sides of mold. Set on baking sheet. Bake in a preheated 350°F oven 8 to 10 minutes, or until golden brown.
4. To remove cookies, tap molds lightly with bottom of a spoon. Cool on a wire rack.

Pennsylvania Dutch Currant Cookies

These delicate cookies, speckled with currants, are a Pennsylvania Dutch Christmas treat. A plain cookie, they make a good contrast to fancier Christmas cookies. *Yields 3–4 dozen*

> 2 *sticks butter*
> 1 *cup granulated sugar*
> ½ *tablespoon grated lemon peel*
> 1 *tablespoon lemon juice*
> 3 *eggs*
> 1¾ *cups all-purpose flour*
> ½ *teaspoon salt*
> ½ *cup currants*
>
> *baking sheet*

1. In a mixing bowl, cream butter and sugar until light and fluffy. Add lemon peel and lemon juice. Mix.

2. Add eggs 1 at a time, beating after each addition. Gradually add flour and salt. Mix thoroughly.

3. Stir in currants. On a large greased baking sheet, drop dough by teaspoonfuls, spreading each thinly with a knife.

4. Bake in a preheated 350°F oven 10 to 15 minutes, until light golden. Cool on a wire rack.

NOTE: Store in an airtight container.

Apees—Pennsylvania Christmas Cookies

These cookies are believed to have been named for one Ann Page, a nineteenth-century cook who stamped her initials on them. A plain flavorful cookie, apees have long been a Christmas treat in Pennsylvania. *Yields 5–6 dozen*

> 1½ *sticks butter*
> 1 *cup granulated sugar*
> 2 *eggs*
> 2½ *cups all-purpose flour*
> ½ *teaspoon baking soda*
> 1 *teaspoon salt*
> ¾ *cup sour cream*
>
> *baking sheet*

1. In a mixing bowl, cream butter and sugar until light and fluffy. Add eggs 1 at a time, beating after each addition.
2. Gradually add dry ingredients, alternating with sour cream. On a lightly greased baking sheet, drop teaspoonfuls of dough 2 inches apart.
3. Bake in a preheated 350°F oven 10 to 15 minutes, or until light brown. Cool on a wire rack.

NOTE: Store in an airtight container.

Hermits

This spicy drop cookie, studded with walnuts, raisins, and citron, is a favorite at Christmastime in the Southern United States. *Yields 6 dozen*

1 *stick butter*
1¼ *cups light brown sugar, firmly packed*
3 *eggs*
2 *cups all-purpose flour*
2 *tablespoons milk*
½ *teaspoon baking soda*
½ *teaspoon ground nutmeg*
1 *tablespoon ground cinnamon*
½ *teaspoon ground cloves*
⅔ *cup coarsely chopped walnuts*
½ *cup golden raisins*
½ *cup finely chopped citron*

baking sheet

1. In a mixing bowl, cream butter and sugar until light and fluffy. Add eggs 1 at a time, beating after each addition. Gradually add flour, milk, baking soda, and spices. Mix.
2. Add nuts, raisins, and citron. Mix thoroughly.
3. Drop a teaspoonful at a time on lightly greased baking sheet. Bake in a preheated 350°F oven 12 to 15 minutes, or until firm to the touch.

NOTE: Store in an airtight container.

Candy Cane Cookies

Few Christmas cookies reflect the holiday more than these. They brighten any Christmas cookie platter and delight children. *Yields about 2 dozen*

> 6 *tablespoons butter*
> ¾ *cup confectioners' sugar*
> 1 *egg*
> ½ *teaspoon almond extract*
> 1 *teaspoon vanilla extract*
> 2 *cups all-purpose flour*
> ½ *teaspoon salt*
> ½ *teaspoon red food coloring*
> 1 *egg white for glaze (optional)*
> *red decorating sugar (optional)*
>
> *baking sheet*

1. In a mixing bowl, cream butter and sugar until light and fluffy. Add egg, almond extract, and vanilla. Mix. Gradually add flour and salt. Mix thoroughly.
2. Divide dough in half and put in two bowls. Add red food coloring to one half, mixing thoroughly.
3. Starting with 1 teaspoon each of red and white dough, roll each piece of dough into a 4-inch rope. Place the red and the white strip alongside each other. Twist together. Place on greased baking sheet. Curve top to form cane handle.
4. If desired, brush with egg white. Sprinkle with red decorating sugar. Bake in a preheated 350°F oven 10 to 12 minutes, or until lightly browned. Cool on a wire rack.

NOTE: Store in an airtight container.

Almond Jumbles

Martha Washington was among the many hostesses in the early days of the United States who served these tasty almond cookies at Christmastime. *Yields 4½ dozen 2-inch cookies*

> 1 stick butter
> 1½ cups confectioners' sugar
> 2 cups all-purpose flour
> 2 egg whites
> 2 cups blanched almonds, finely ground
> ⅓ cup light cream
> 2 teaspoons rosewater
> confectioners' sugar for sprinkling on top
>
> 2-inch round cookie cutters; baking sheet

1. In a mixing bowl, cream butter and sugar until light and fluffy. Gradually add flour, egg whites, almonds, light cream, and rosewater. Mix thoroughly. Refrigerate dough overnight.
2. On a lightly floured surface, roll dough to ⅛-inch thickness. With cookie cutters, cut out circles. Place on greased baking sheet. Prick each circle several times with a fork.
3. Place in a preheated 350°F oven 8 to 10 minutes, or until lightly browned. Cool on a wire rack. Sprinkle freely with confectioners' sugar.

NOTES: Store in an airtight container.

If desired, sprinkle again with confectioners' sugar again before serving.

Stained Glass Windows

One of the most handsome cookies, stained glass windows are as good to look at as they are to eat. You can enjoy viewing their sour-ball (or Life Saver) panes on a Christmas tree or in a window. Or you can serve the cookies to guests as a treat. *Yields 2 dozen*

1 *stick butter*
½ *cup granulated sugar*
¼ *cup light molasses*
1 *teaspoon baking soda*
½ *teaspoon salt*
2½ *cups flour*
¼ *cup water*

Filling
3 *6-ounce packages sour balls*
or
6 *packages Life Savers, different colors*

baking sheet covered with aluminum foil

1. In a mixing bowl, cream butter and sugar until light and fluffy. Add remaining batter ingredients. Mix. Refrigerate at least 1 hour.

2. Sort candies by color. Place each color in a separate dish towel or a plastic bag (the bag may have to be replaced as it gets punctured). Using a hammer, crush balls coarsely (if too fine, candy will lose transparency during baking).

3. Lightly grease foil in baking sheet. With a pointed instrument, trace outline of cookie shapes on foil. Roll out dough in ¼-inch strips. Lay strips along outlines. (If you wish to place divisions within outlines, do so now.) Fill in with crushed candies just high enough to cover spaces. Don't mix colors.

4. Bake in a preheated 350°F oven 6 to 9 minutes, or until candy has melted. Poke a hole in the top of each cookie to be used

as an ornament and bake this only 3 minutes. After baking, make sure hole is still open. Cool 20 minutes before removing foil.

Bourbon Balls

Tangy and rich, these bourbon-drenched balls are a perfect Christmas delicacy—just the tidbit to round off a day of feasting! *Yields about 5 dozen*

> 1 *cup confectioners' sugar*
> 2 *cups graham crackers, finely ground*
> 2½ *tablespoons cocoa*
> 1 *tablespoon grated orange rind*
> 1 *cup finely chopped pecans*
> 3 *tablespoons light corn syrup*
> ¼ *cup bourbon*
> *confectioners' sugar for coating*
>
> *plate*

1. In a mixing bowl, combine sugar, graham cracker crumbs, cocoa, orange rind, and pecans. Toss. Add corn syrup and bourbon; mix thoroughly.
2. Form 1-inch balls. Roll in sugar until coated.

NOTES: Store in an airtight container.

Tastes best when allowed to mellow for several days.

Acadian Lep Kuchen

The French Cajuns adapted the German recipe Lebkuchen (see page 194) to produce this spicy cookie, a favorite at Christmastime in Acadia. *Yields about 3 dozen*

> 2½ cups all-purpose flour
> 1 teaspoon baking powder
> ½ tablespoon ground cinnamon
> ½ tablespoon ground nutmeg
> ½ tablespoon ground allspice
> 5 eggs
> ¾ cup granulated sugar
> ¾ cup light corn syrup
> 2 1-ounce squares sweetened chocolate, melted
> ¼ teaspoon salt
> 1 teaspoon vanilla extract
> ½ cup coarsely chopped citron
> ½ cup golden raisins
> ¾ cup chopped unblanched almonds.

> **Icing**
> 2 egg whites
> 1 cup confectioners' sugar
> 1 teaspoon almond extract

> 15½ × 10½ × 1-inch pan

1. In a small bowl, combine flour, baking powder, and spices. Reserve ¼ cup of flour mixture. In a mixing bowl, beat eggs and sugar until light and fluffy. Add corn syrup, chocolate, salt, and vanilla. Mix thoroughly.

2. Mix reserved flour mixture with citron, raisins, and almonds. Fold into batter. Grease pan and pour in batter.

3. Bake in a preheated 350°F oven about 10 minutes, or until a cake tester comes out clean.

4. Combine icing ingredients. Ice cake while still warm. When cool, cut into bars.

Irish Christmas Cookies

These festive cookies are fortified with Irish whiskey. A favorite in Ireland at Christmastime, they make a hit anywhere. *Yields about 5 dozen*

> 2 sticks butter
> 1⅓ cups granulated sugar
> 2 eggs
> 2¾ cups all-purpose flour
> ⅓ cup Irish whiskey
> ⅓ cup dark raisins
> ⅓ cup chopped blanched almonds
> ⅓ cup candied citron, coarsely chopped
>
> baking sheet

1. In a mixing bowl, cream butter and sugar until light and fluffy. Add eggs 1 at a time, beating after each addition.
2. Gradually add flour. Add whiskey, raisins, almonds, and citron. Mix thoroughly.
3. Drop batter on greased baking sheet, 1 teaspoon at a time. Bake in a preheated 350°F oven about 8 minutes, or until edges are a light brown. Remove to a wire rack immediately.

NOTE: Store in an airtight container

Springerle Cookies

(SPRING-er-lee)

These anise-flavored cookies are shaped by a special rolling pin or a board that presses Christmas designs (often including the Springerle or vaulting horse) into the cookies. Enjoyed for centuries in Germany, Springerle have become a universal Christmas favorite. *Yields about 3–4 dozen*

> 2 eggs
> 1 cup sifted confectioners' sugar
> 1 teaspoon grated lemon peel
> 2¾ cups all-purpose flour
> aniseeds
>
> *springerle rolling pin and board (available*
> *in most gourmet shops); baking sheet*

1. In a mixing bowl, mix eggs, sugar, and lemon peel. Gradually add flour, mixing thoroughly.
2. On a lightly floured surface, knead dough until smooth. Roll out on a lightly floured surface to ¼-inch thickness. Dust springerle rolling pin or board lightly with flour.
3. Roll springerle rolling pin firmly over dough or press board on dough. With a floured knife, cut cookies apart. Grease baking sheet and sprinkle with aniseeds.
4. Brush off any excess flour from cookies. Place cookies, design side up, on prepared baking sheet. Cover with towel and leave at room temperature 8 hours or overnight.
5. Bake in a preheated 300°F oven 12 to 15 minutes, or until a light straw color.

NOTE: Will mellow if stored in an airtight container for up to 3 weeks.

Spritz Cookies

A Christmas treat in Scandinavia and Germany, these butter cookies are as festive in appearance as they are in flavor. Use a cookie press to shape the spritz into stars, wreaths, trees, and other Christmas designs. *Yields about 4 dozen*

> ½ *stick butter*
> ½ *cup granulated sugar*
> 1 *egg*
> ½ *teaspoon vanilla extract*
> 1 *teaspoon grated lemon peel*
> 2⅓ *cups all-purpose flour*
> *food coloring or colored sugar (optional)*
>
> *cookie press; baking sheet*

1. In a mixing bowl, cream butter and sugar until light and fluffy. Add egg, vanilla, and lemon peel. Mix.
2. Gradually add flour. Add food coloring if desired. Mix thoroughly.
3. Fill cookie press half full of dough and press out cookies in desired shapes on ungreased baking sheet. Sprinkle colored sugar lightly on cookies if desired.
4. Bake in a preheated 350°F oven 10 to 12 minutes, or until edges are a light brown.

NOTE: Store in an airtight container.

Lebkuchen—German Honey Cake

(LAPE-koo-ken)

These cookies have been a specialty of bakers in Nuremberg, Germany, for centuries—developed when honey rather than sugar was the main sweetener. A favorite for Christmas, Lebkuchen in the shape of hearts are also a big favorite for Valentine's Day. *Yields 2–3 dozen*

2 tablespoons butter, softened
2½ cups all-purpose flour
½ teaspoon baking powder
¼ teaspoon ground cloves
¼ teaspoon ground cinnamon
¼ teaspoon ground nutmeg
¼ teaspoon ground allspice
⅓ cup candied lemon peel, finely chopped
⅓ cup candied orange peel, finely chopped
½ cup unbleached almonds, finely chopped
1 egg
½ cup dark brown sugar, firmly packed
1½ cups dark molasses
½ cup honey

Glaze
1 egg white
1 tablespoon lemon juice
1 teaspoon lemon peel
1 cup confectioners' sugar

15½ × 10½ × 1-inch pan

1. Grease pan. Sprinkle lightly with flour.
2. In a small mixing bowl, combine flour, baking powder, spices, fruit peels, and almonds.
3. In another mixing bowl, cream egg and brown sugar until

light and fluffy. Stir in molasses and honey. Gradually add dry ingredients. Mix thoroughly.

4. Pour batter into prepared pan. Bake in a preheated 350°F oven 15 to 20 minutes, or until a cake tester comes out clean.

5. While cake is baking, make glaze. Combine egg white, lemon juice and peel, and sugar.

6. While cake is warm, brush with glaze. Wait a couple of minutes until glaze hardens slightly. Cut into 2 by 1-inch bars. Cool on a wire rack.

NOTE: Store in an airtight container up to 8 weeks.

Mandelkranzchen—German Almond Wreaths

(MAHN-del-KRAHNZ-ken)

With both eye appeal and a delicate almond flavor, these wreath-shaped cookies are a favorite in Germany at Christmastime. *Yields about 2 dozen*

> 1 stick butter
> 1/3 cup granulated sugar
> 1 egg
> 2 teaspoons grated lemon peel
> 1¾ cups all-purpose flour
> 1 egg yolk beaten with 1 tablespoon water for glaze
> blanched almonds, finely chopped
>
> wreath cookie cutter; baking sheet

1. In a mixing bowl, cream butter and sugar until light and fluffy. Add egg, lemon peel, and gradually the flour. Mix thoroughly. Chill dough overnight.

2. Roll out dough to ⅛-inch thickness. Cut out cookies with wreath cookie cutter, or use a 2-inch round cutter and cut out centers. Place on lightly greased baking sheet.

3. Brush with egg yolk mixture. Sprinkle lightly with almonds. Bake in a preheated 350°F oven about 10 to 15 minutes, or until lightly browned. Cool on a wire rack.

NOTE: Store in an airtight container.

Zimsterne—Cinnamon Stars

(TSIM-shtern-eh)

In Germany and Austria, these crunchy cookies are a tremendous favorite at Christmastime. *Yields about 4 dozen*

> *3 egg whites*
> *1½ cups confectioners' sugar*
> *1½ tablespoons ground cinnamon*
> *1 teaspoon grated lemon rind*
> *2 cups unblanched almonds, finely ground*
>
> *2-inch star cookie cutter; baking sheet*

1. In a mixing bowl, beat egg whites until foamy. Gradually add sugar. Beat until very stiff, about 10 minutes. Reserve ½ cup.

2. Add cinnamon, lemon rind, and almonds. Mix thoroughly. Add more finely ground almonds if dough is not thick enough (or too sticky) to roll out.

3. Sprinkle a pastry board with finely ground almonds. Roll out dough to ¼-inch thickness. Cut out stars with cookie cutter. Place on lightly greased baking sheet. Brush stars with ½ cup of reserved egg white mixture.

4. Bake in a preheated 300°F oven 20 to 25 minutes, or until golden brown. Cool on baking sheet.

NOTES: Store in an airtight container.

Tastes best when allowed to mellow 2 to 3 weeks.

To soften cookies that have become hard, store with a slice of bread or a slice of apple.

Berlinerkranser—Norwegian "Berlin" Wreaths

(behr-LEEN-er-KRAHNZ-er)

These butter cookie wreaths, originating in Norway, have become beloved favorites in the Christmas celebrations of many countries. Glittering with sugar, they adorn any plate of Christmas cookies. *Yields 4–5 dozen*

>2 sticks butter
>$^2/_3$ cup granulated sugar
>$^1/_2$ tablespoon grated orange peel
>2 eggs
>2 tablespoons brandy
>$3^2/_3$ cups all-purpose flour
>2 egg whites for glaze
>$^2/_3$ cup cube sugar for sprinkling on top
>
>baking sheet

1. In a mixing bowl, cream butter, sugar, and orange peel until light and fluffy. Add eggs 1 at a time, beating after each addition.

2. Add brandy and gradually the flour. Refrigerate dough overnight.

3. Roll small pieces of dough into strips 6 inches long and ¼ inch thick. Form each into a circle, passing one end over and through to make a single knot. Ends should stick out ½ inch on each side.

4. Place on ungreased baking sheet. Beat egg whites lightly. Brush on top of cookies. In a small bowl, coarsely crush cube sugar. Sprinkle on top of each cookie.

5. Bake in a preheated 350°F oven 10 to 12 minutes, or until golden brown. Cool on a wire rack.

NOTE: Store in an airtight container.

Bentheimer Moppen—Christmas Honey Cookies

These little cookies, a Christmas tradition in Bentheim, West Germany, are a blend of cinnamon, cloves, and almond flavors, with a lemon frosting. *Yields 6 dozen*

> ¾ cup honey
> ½ stick butter
> 1 egg
> ½ cup granulated sugar
> 1 teaspoon ground cinnamon
> 1 teaspoon ground cloves
> 3¼ cups all-purpose flour
> ½ tablespoon baking powder
> ⅓ cup finely chopped almonds
>
> **Frosting**
> 1 tablespoon lemon juice
> 1¾ cups confectioners' sugar
> 1 tablespoon water
>
> baking sheet

1. In a saucepan, melt honey and butter. Cool. Add egg and sugar. Beat together.
2. Add remaining ingredients. Mix. *Chill dough 3 days.*
3. Shape dough into walnut-size balls. Place on lightly greased baking sheet. Bake in a preheated 350°F oven 8 to 12 minutes, or until golden brown. Cool on baking sheet 2 minutes. Continue cooling on a wire rack.
4. To make frosting: In a bowl, combine lemon juice, sugar, and water. Dip each cookie in the bowl.

NOTES: Wait 1 day before serving.
   Store in an airtight container.

Pfeffernüsse—German "Peppernuts"

(FEFF-er-noo-seh)

These spicy drop cookies have long been Christmas favorites in Germany and the Scandinavian countries. Their lively flavor makes them a welcome addition to the Christmas cookie plate. *Yields 5–6 dozen*

2½ cups flour
¼ teaspoon baking powder
¼ teaspooon ground cinnamon
¼ teaspoon ground cloves
¼ teaspoon ground allspice
⅛ teaspoon black pepper
¼ cup honey
⅓ cup dark corn syrup
¼ cup granulated sugar
3 tablespoons butter

baking sheet

1. In a mixing bowl, combine flour, baking powder, spices, and pepper. Mix. Set aside.

2. In a saucepan, combine honey, corn syrup, and sugar. Place over medium heat, stirring until sugar is dissolved. Reduce heat. Add butter and stir until butter is melted. Remove from heat; cool slightly.

3. Gradually add to dry ingredients. Mix thoroughly. Refrigerate overnight.

4. Shape dough into 1-inch balls. Bake on greased baking sheet in a 325°F oven 12 to 15 minutes, or until lightly browned. Cool on a wire rack.

NOTES: Store 6 to 8 weeks in an airtight container.

If desired, place ¼ of an apple in the container to keep cookies soft; replace when necessary.

Mailänderli—Swiss Christmas Butter Cookies

(MY-LEND-er-lee)

The name comes from Milan, but the cookies are a Christmas tradition in Switzerland. For many Swiss, no Christmas would be complete without these butter cookies. *Yields about 2½ dozen*

> 1 stick butter
> ½ cup granulated sugar
> 1 tablespoon grated lemon rind
> 2 tablespoons lemon juice
> 2 eggs
> 2½ cups all-purpose flour
> granulated sugar for sprinkling on top (optional)
>
> 2-inch cookie cutters; baking sheet

    1. In a mixing bowl, cream butter and sugar until light and fluffy. Add lemon rind, lemon juice, and eggs. Mix.
    2. Add flour gradually. Mix thoroughly. Refrigerate at least 1 hour.
    3. On a lightly floured surface, roll out dough to ⅛-inch thickness. Using 2-inch cookie cutters—such as stars, bells, and trees—cut out cookies. Place on lightly greased baking sheet.
    4. Bake in a preheated 350°F oven 10 to 15 minutes, or until lightly browned. Cool on a wire rack. Sprinkle with sugar if desired.

NOTE: Store in an airtight container. Cookies mellow with age.

Basler Leckerli—Basel Honey Cookies

(BAHS-ler LECK-er-lee)

This honey cookie comes from Basel, Switzerland. For centuries, the Swiss have cherished Leckerli as a treat that epitomizes Christmas. *Yields about 4 dozen*

$\frac{1}{4}$ *cup candied orange peel, finely chopped*
$\frac{1}{4}$ *cup candied lemon peel, finely chopped*
$\frac{1}{2}$ *cup kirsch*
$\frac{1}{2}$ *cup honey*
1 *cup granulated sugar*
$2\frac{3}{4}$ *cups all-purpose flour*
1 *teaspoon baking powder*
1 *teaspoon ground cinnamon*
$\frac{1}{2}$ *teaspoon ground cloves*
$\frac{1}{2}$ *teaspoon ground nutmeg*
$\frac{3}{4}$ *cup unblanched almonds, finely ground*

Glaze
1 *cup confectioners' sugar*
1–2 *tablespoons water*
$\frac{1}{2}$ *teaspoon lemon extract*

baking sheet

1. Soak fruit peels in kirsch about 30 minutes. In a saucepan, heat honey and sugar until well melted, but not boiling. Remove from heat.

2. Add remaining batter ingredients. Mix thoroughly. Cover dough and allow to mellow at room temperature 2 days to 1 week.

3. On a lightly floured surface, roll out dough to $\frac{1}{2}$-inch thickness. Cut into bars about 2 by 3 inches. Place bars on lightly greased baking sheet.

4. Bake in a preheated 350°F oven 20 to 25 minutes, or until golden brown.

5. To make glaze: In a bowl, combine sugar, water, and

lemon extract. Place bars on a wire rack. While warm, brush bars with glaze.

NOTE: Store in an airtight container and allow to mellow for about 1 month.

Basler Brunsli—Swiss Christmas Cookies

(BAHS-ler BRUNS-lee)

A tradition at Christmas in Switzerland, these almond-cocoa cookies (originating in Basel) make any occasion festive. *Yields about 5 dozen*

> 1½ cups unblanched almonds, finely ground
> 1 cup granulated sugar
> 1½ tablespoons cocoa
> 1 tablespoon ground cinnamon
> 2 tablespoons cognac
> 2 eggs
> 1 cup flour
> granulated sugar for sprinkling on top
>
> 2-inch round cookie cutter; baking sheet

1. In a bowl, combine almonds, sugar, cocoa, and cinnamon. Mix. Add cognac, eggs, and flour. Mix thoroughly. Chill overnight.
2. On a lightly sugared surface, roll out dough to ¼-inch thickness. With cookie cutter, cut out cookies. Sprinkle sugar on top of cookies.
3. Place on greased baking sheet. Leave on counter overnight. Bake in a preheated 300°F oven 15 to 20 minutes, or until done. Cool on a wire rack.

NOTE: Store in an airtight container.

Gevülde Speculaas—Dutch Christmas Cookies

(he-VULD-e SPECK-oo-laws)

These spicy squares, each topped with an almond, are an old-fashioned Christmas treat in Holland. Their unpretentious goodness makes them a constant favorite. They will keep indefinitely in the refrigerator, if someone doesn't discover them first. *Yields 36 squares*

2½ cups all-purpose flour
1 teaspoon baking powder
1 cup dark brown sugar, firmly packed
½ tablespoon ground cinnamon
1 teaspoon ground cloves
1 teaspoon ground nutmeg
½ teaspoon ground cardamom
1 stick butter
1 cup milk
½ cup almond paste
1 egg
1 egg beaten with 1 tablespoon water for glaze
sliced blanched almonds

8 × 8-inch pan

1. In a mixing bowl, combine flour, baking powder, sugar, and spices. Add butter and milk. Mix thoroughly. Set aside.

2. Combine almond paste with 1 egg. Mix thoroughly. Grease pan. Press ⅓ of dough in bottom. Spread almond paste on top of dough. Cover with remaining dough.

3. Brush top of dough with egg-and-water mixture. Score top into 36 squares (for positioning of almonds). Place an almond slice in each square. Brush again with egg-and-water mixture.

4. Bake in a preheated 350°F oven about 50 minutes, or until a cake tester comes out clean. Cool on a wire rack.

NOTE: These freeze well.

Mormors' Syltkakor— Grandmother's Jelly Cookies

(MOR-mers SULT-kak-er)

A Christmas treat from Sweden, this two-layered Christmas cookie has a currant jelly filling that lends it a distinctive tang. A very special cookie. *Yields 2½ dozen*

> 2 *sticks butter*
> ⅔ *cup granulated sugar*
> 1 *egg*
> 2½ *cups all-purpose flour*
> ¼ *teaspoon salt*
> 2 *tablespoons blanched almonds, finely chopped*
> 2 *tablespoons granulated sugar*
> 1 *egg white*
> *currant jelly*
>
> 2½-*inch round cookie cutter; 2-inch scalloped*
> *round cookie cutter; thimble or round*
> *cookie cutter of similar size; baking sheet*

1. In a mixing bowl, cream butter and sugar until light and fluffy. Add egg, flour, and salt. Mix thoroughly.

2. On a lightly floured surface, roll out dough to ⅛-inch thickness. With 2½-inch cookie cutter, cut out 30 rounds. With 2-inch cookie cutter, cut out another 30 rounds. Using a thimble or a small cookie cutter, cut holes in center of 2-inch rounds.

3. In a small mixing bowl, combine almonds and sugar. Set aside. Brush 2-inch rounds with egg white. Sprinkle with almond-sugar mixture.

4. Place rounds on lightly greased baking sheet. Bake in a preheated 375°F oven 10 to 12 minutes, or until light brown. Cool on a wire rack.

5. In the center of each 2½-inch cookie, place 1 teaspoonful

of currant jelly. Place a 2-inch cookie, almond side up, on each 2½-inch cookie. Press together gently. (Jelly should show through the center of the top cookie.)

Konjakskransar—Swedish Brandy Rings

(KOHN-yak-KRAHN-sar)

These brandy-flavored cookies twisted into rings will add a touch of Sweden to your Christmas. They look festive on a plate and are delicious with coffee. *Yields about 2 dozen*

> 2 *sticks butter*
> ½ *cup confectioners' sugar*
> 3 *tablespoons brandy*
> 3 *cups all-purpose flour*
>
> *baking sheet*

1. In a mixing bowl, cream butter and sugar until light and fluffy. Add brandy and gradually the flour. Mix thoroughly.
2. Roll out dough into pencil-thin ropes each 5 inches long. Twist two ropes together and join ends to form a ring.
3. Place rings on lightly greased baking sheet. Bake in a preheated 350°F oven 10 to 15 minutes, or until golden brown. Leave on baking sheet about 5 minutes. Then cool on a wire rack.

NOTE: Store in an airtight container.

Rum Balls

These tangy cookies make a nice contrast to milder cookies—one reason for their popularity. *Yields about 3 dozen walnut-size balls*

> 2½ *cups vanilla wafers, finely chopped*
> 1 *cup walnuts, finely chopped*
> 1¼ *cups sifted confectioners' sugar*
> 3 *tablespoons sifted cocoa powder*
> ¼ *teaspoon salt*
> ⅓ *cup rum*
> 2 *tablespoons dark corn syrup*
> *confectioners' sugar for coating*
>
> *baking sheet*

1. In a mixing bowl, mix together vanilla wafers, walnuts, sugar, cocoa powder, and salt. Add rum and corn syrup. Mix thoroughly.

2. Cover baking sheet or plate with wax paper. Form dough into walnut-size balls. Roll balls in confectioners' sugar. Place on paper. Put in cool place for a day. (Leaving it for a week will bring out the flavor even more.)

NOTE: Before serving, reroll balls in confectioners' sugar.

Finnska Pinnar—Swedish Finnish Fingers

The Swedes call this butter cookie "Finnish" after their neighbor to the east. Whatever its national origins, the fingers are one of the featured cookies at Swedish Christmas parties. *Yields 4–5 dozen*

>   2 *sticks butter*
>   1/4 *cup granulated sugar*
>   1/2 *cup blanched almonds, finely ground*
>   2 *cups all-purpose flour*
>   1/4 *teaspoon salt*
>   1 *teaspoon almond extract*
>   1/2 *teaspoon lemon extract*
>   1 *teaspoon vanilla extract*
>   1 *egg white for glaze*
>   *sugar for dipping*
>
>   *baking sheet*

1. In a mixing bowl, cream butter and sugar until light and fluffy. Add almonds. Gradually add flour, salt, and almond, lemon, and vanilla extracts. Mix thoroughly. Refrigerate dough overnight.

2. On a lightly floured surface, roll out dough to 1/8-inch thickness. Cut into 2-inch squares. For rolling, place sugar on a plate. Brush egg white on cookies and dip into sugar. Roll up, jelly-roll style.

3. Place on greased baking sheet 2 inches apart. Bake in a preheated 350°F oven 10 to 15 minutes, or until slightly browned at the ends. Cool on a wire rack.

NOTE: Store in an airtight container.

Julestjerner—Danish Christmas Stars

(YUL-e-STYAHN-nah)

These molasses cookies are a never-failing hit at Christmastime. Their flavor appeals to people of all ages, but children especially return to them again and again. Long a favorite on Danish Christmas sideboards, they will be on yours too. *Yields 5–6 dozen*

> 1 teaspoon lemon juice
> ¾ cup milk
> 4½ cups all-purpose flour
> 1 teaspoon baking soda
> ½ tablespoon ground cinnamon
> ½ tablespoon salt
> 2 sticks butter
> 1 cup molasses
>
> *2½–3-inch star cookie cutter; baking sheet*

1. In a cup, add lemon juice to milk. Mix. In a bowl, combine milk, flour, baking soda, cinnamon, and salt. Set aside.
2. In a mixing bowl, cream butter. Slowly add molasses. Mix. Gradually add flour mixture. Mix thoroughly. (Dough will be stiff.) Chill 1 hour.
3. On a lightly floured surface, roll out dough to ¼-inch thickness. Cut stars with cookie cutter. Place on baking sheet.
4. Bake in a preheated 350°F oven 10 to 15 minutes, or until firm. Cool on a wire rack.

NOTE: Store in an airtight container.

Vanillekranse—Danish Vanilla Wreaths

(va-NEE-ye-KRAHN-se)

These wreath-shaped cookies, flavored with vanilla and almonds, are a perennial Christmas treat from Denmark. *Yields 3 dozen*

> 2 *sticks butter*
> ³/₄ *cup granulated sugar*
> 2 *eggs*
> 1 *teaspoon vanilla extract*
> 2²/₃ *cups all-purpose flour*
> ¹/₂ *teaspoon baking powder*
> ¹/₄ *teaspoon salt*
> ¹/₂ *cup blanched almonds, finely ground*
> *vanilla sugar for coating (see page 5)*
>
> *baking sheet*

1. In a mixing bowl, cream butter and sugar until light and fluffy. Add eggs and vanilla. Mix.
2. Gradually add flour, baking powder, salt, and almonds. Mix. Chill 1 hour.
3. Using 1 tablespoon of dough, make a rope ¼ inch thick and 3 inches long. Shape into a circle and overlap ends. Place on greased baking sheet.
4. Bake in a preheated 325°F oven 15 to 20 minutes, or until golden brown. While still hot, roll in vanilla sugar. Cool on a wire rack.

NOTE: Store in an airtight container.

Nissu Nassu—Finnish Christmas Pigs

(NES-soo NUS-soo)

The appearance of these pig-shaped cookies in Finland is a sign that Christmas is near. They are so fragrant and tasty—with or without frosting—that everyone looks forward to them as a special treat. *Yields about 4 dozen*

2½ cups all-purpose flour
½ tablespoon baking soda
1 tablespoon ground cinnamon
½ tablespoon ground ginger
½ tablespoon ground cloves
1 stick butter
1 cup light brown sugar, firmly packed
1 cup water

Icing (optional)
1 cup confectioners' sugar
1 tablespoon butter
½ teaspoon vanilla extract
1–2 tablespoons water

pig-shaped cookie cutter; baking sheet;
pastry bag with thin writing tube

1. In a bowl, combine flour, baking soda, and spices. Mix. Set aside.

2. In a mixing bowl, cream butter and sugar until light and fluffy. Gradually add dry ingredients. Add water 1 tablespoon at a time. Chill at least 2 hours.

3. On a lightly floured surface, roll out dough to ⅛-inch thickness. With cookie cutter, cut out pigs. Place on lightly greased baking sheet.

4. Bake in a preheated 375°F oven 8 to 12 minutes, or until lightly brown. Cool on a wire rack.

5. To make frosting: In a mixing bowl, mix sugar, butter, and vanilla. Add enough water so mixture can be drizzled on cookies. Using pastry bag, frost cookies. If you wish, outline pigs with a dot for the eye, or write the names of guests on them.

Ruiskakkuja—Finnish Rye Cookies

(ROOEES-KUK-ku-ya)

Tangy with rye, these cookies are a favorite at Christmas celebrations in Finland. Their circular shape with an off-center hole imitates the standard Finnish sour rye bread. *Yields about 2 dozen*

> 1 *stick butter*
> ¼ *cup confectioners' sugar*
> 1 *cup rye flour*
> ½ *cup all-purpose flour*
>
> *3-inch round cookie cutter; 1-inch round cookie cutter; baking sheet*

1. In a mixing bowl, cream butter and sugar until light and fluffy. Gradually add flours. Knead until smooth, about 5 minutes.

2. On a lightly floured surface, roll out dough to ⅛-inch thickness. Using a 3-inch round cookie cutter, cut out cookies. With a very small round cutter or bottle cap (about 1 inch across), cut a hole slightly off-center. Place on lightly greased baking sheet.

3. Using a fork, make several pricks in cookies. Bake in a preheated 375°F oven about 8 minutes, or until lightly browned. Cool on a wire rack.

NOTE: Store in an airtight container.

Belgian Christmas Cookies

The flavor of almonds suffuses these traditional Christmas cookies. Top with red and green sugar to lend them holiday hues.
Yields about 8 dozen

> 2½ *cups all-purpose flour*
> 2 *teaspoons baking powder*
> ¼ *teaspoon salt*
> 2 *sticks butter*
> 1½ *cups dark brown sugar, firmly packed*
> 1 *teaspoon almond extract*
> 4 *eggs*
> 1 *cup unblanched almonds, finely chopped*
> 1 *tablespoon ground cinnamon*
> 2 *tablespoons red sugar*
> 2 *tablespoons green sugar*
>
> *17 × 11 × 1-inch jelly-roll pan*

1. In a bowl, combine flour, baking powder, and salt. Mix.
Set aside.

2. In a mixing bowl, cream butter and sugar until light and
fluffy. Add almond extract and eggs 1 at a time, beating after each
addition. Gradually add flour mixture and mix thoroughly.

3. Place in greased pan. Mix together almonds and cinnamon.
Sprinkle on top of batter. Mix red and green sugars. Sprinkle on
batter.

4. Bake in a 375°F oven 10 to 15 minutes, or until a cake
tester comes out clean. Cut into 1 by 2-inch bars while warm.

Amaretti—Italian Almond Macaroons

These almond delicacies, originating in Italy, have become international favorites. They are crisp on the outside and chewy inside. Wrapped in colored papers or served on a platter with other cookies favored at Christmastime, amaretti always add a festive touch to the celebration of the season. *Yields about 2 dozen*

> 2 *egg whites*
> 1 *teaspoon almond extract*
> ½ *tablespoon grated lemon rind*
> 1½ *cups blanched almonds, finely chopped*
> 2 *cups confectioners' sugar plus sugar for sprinkling*
>   *on top*
>
> *baking sheet*

1. In a mixing bowl, beat egg whites until stiff peaks stand up. Add almond extract and lemon rind. Mix. Gradually add almonds and sugar, mixing thoroughly.
2. Line pan with foil or parchment paper. Drop teaspoonfuls of dough 1 inch apart on ungreased baking sheet. Flatten slightly with palm of hand.
3. Sprinkle lightly with confectioners' sugar. Let stand 2 or 3 hours in a cool place.
4. Bake in a preheated 350°F oven about 20 minutes, or until golden brown. Do not overbake. Cool on a wire rack.

NOTE: Store in an airtight container.

Pastini di Natale—Italian Christmas Cookies

(pahs-TEE-ni dee nah-TAH-lay)

These frosted cookies are an Italian delicacy that brightens the Christmas table. *Yields about 3 dozen*

2¾ cups all-purpose flour
¼ teaspoon salt
½ tablespoon baking powder
2 sticks butter
¾ cup granulated sugar
1½ tablespoons grated lemon rind
2 eggs

Lemon Icing
3 cups sifted confectioners' sugar
1 tablespoon lemon juice
4–5 tablespoons water
candied cherries (optional)
chopped pistachio nuts (optional)

2-inch cookie cutters; baking sheet

1. In a small bowl, combine flour, salt, and baking powder. Set aside. In a mixing bowl, cream butter and sugar until light and fluffy.

2. Add lemon rind and eggs. Mix. Gradually add flour mixture. Mix thoroughly. Refrigerate at least 1 hour.

3. On a lightly floured surface, roll out dough to ⅛-inch thickness. Using 2-inch cookie cutters—such as bells, wreaths, and candles—cut out cookies. Place on lightly greased baking sheet.

4. Bake in a preheated 350°F oven 10 to 15 minutes, or until lightly browned. Cool on a wire rack.

5. Combine ingredients for icing. Mix thoroughly. Decorate cookies with icing and candied cherries and nuts.

NOTE: Store in an airtight container after frosting hardens.

Kourabiedes—Greek Butter Cookies

(kou-rah-bi-AH-thes)

Popular on many festive occasions in Greece, these cookies are a favorite at Christmas. At this time, a clove is placed in each cookie to commemorate the spices the Wise Men offered to the Christ Child. *Yields about 3 dozen*

> 1 *stick butter, softened*
> ½ *cup sifted confectioners' sugar*
> 2 *egg yolks*
> 3 *tablespoons cognac*
> 1 *teaspoon vanilla extract*
> 2¼ *cups all-purpose flour*
> *whole cloves*
> *sifted confectioners' sugar for sprinkling on top*
>
> *baking sheet*

1. In a mixing bowl, cream butter and sugar until light and fluffy. Beat in egg yolks, cognac, and vanilla.

2. Gradually add enough flour to make a stiff dough. Knead dough until smooth. Shape into 1-inch balls and insert a whole clove into each. Place on ungreased baking sheet.

3. Bake in a preheated 350°F oven about 20 minutes, or until light golden. Cool on a wire rack. Sift confectioners' sugar generously over the cookies when cooled.

Grybai—Lithuanian Mushroom Cookies

(GREE-bye)

Mushrooms, so dear to the peoples of the Baltic as well as those of Eastern Europe, are recognized in these charming Christmas spice cookies—mushroom in shape if not in content. *Yields 5½ dozen*

1 cup honey
½ stick butter
⅓ cup granulated sugar
2 eggs
¼ cup sour cream
4⅓ cups all-purpose flour
½ tablespoon baking soda
½ tablespoon ground cinnamon
1 teaspoon ground cardamom
1 teaspoon ground cloves
1 teaspoon ground ginger
1 teaspoon ground nutmeg
½ tablespoon grated lemon rind
½ tablespoon grated orange rind

Icing
3 cups confectioners' sugar
¼ cup water
2–3 tablespoons lemon juice
1 tablespoon unsweetened cocoa

baking sheets

1. In a saucepan, heat honey. Cool to lukewarm. In a mixing bowl, cream butter and sugar until light and fluffy. Add eggs 1 at a time, beating after each addition. Add sour cream and honey. Mix.

2. In a mixing bowl, combine flour, baking soda, spices, and

fruit rinds. Add flour mixture to batter ½ cup at a time. Refrigerate dough overnight.

3. Cut off ½ of dough. Pull off walnut-size pieces. Shape into balls of varying size. Indenting with finger, mold into mushroom caps. Set on greased baking sheet. Bake in a preheated 350°F oven 10 to 15 minutes, or until lightly firm. (When cookies are done, you may have to press your finger into the holes of the caps to keep them open.)

4. Make stems of remaining dough: Roll small pieces into ropes about ½ inch thick. Cut into varying lengths of 1 to 1½ inches, with one end slightly tapered. Place on greased baking sheet. Bake 7 to 10 minutes, or until lightly firm. Cool on a wire rack.

5. To make icing: Beat together confectioners' sugar, water, and lemon juice. Divide icing in half. Mix cocoa into one of the halves.

6. To assemble: Dip stems into icing; coat evenly. Press tapered end of stem into mushroom cap. Place mushrooms cap side down on wax paper to dry.

7. When dry, dip mushroom caps in cocoa icing. Place on sides on wax paper and allow to dry.

Polish Poppyseed Cookies

This butter cookie garnished with poppyseeds, a Polish Christmas treat, is simple but elegant. *Yields 4 dozen*

> 2 *sticks butter*
> ⅔ *cup granulated sugar*
> 1 *teaspoon vanilla extract*
> 3 *hard-boiled egg yolks, sieved*
> 2 *egg yolks*
> 2¼ *cups all-purpose flour*
> ¼ *teaspoon salt*
> 1 *egg beaten with 1 tablespoon water for glaze*
> *poppyseeds for sprinkling on top*
>
> *2-inch round cookie cutter; baking sheet*

1. In a mixing bowl, cream butter and sugar until light and fluffy. Add vanilla, hard-boiled and raw egg yolks, flour, and salt. Mix thoroughly. Refrigerate dough at least 1 hour.

2. On a lightly floured surface, roll out dough to ¼-inch thickness. Cut into rounds with cookie cutter. Place on lightly greased baking sheet.

3. Brush tops with egg-and-water glaze. Sprinkle lightly with poppyseeds. Bake in a preheated 350°F oven 10 to 12 minutes, or until golden brown.

NOTE: Store in an airtight container.

Medeni Kurabii—Bulgarian Honey Cookies

(MEH-de-nee koo-ra-BEE)

These honey cookies, a Christmas tradition in Bulgaria, are easy to make and a sure favorite at any festive gathering. *Yields 2–3 dozen*

>1 *stick butter*
>¼ *cup honey*
>¾ *cup confectioners' sugar*
>½ *teaspoon baking soda*
>1 *egg*
>2 *cups all-purpose flour*
>⅔ *cup cube sugar*
>
>*baking sheet*

1. In a mixing bowl, combine butter, honey, sugar, baking soda, and egg. Mix. Gradually add flour. Mix thoroughly.

2. Shape into balls, 1 teaspoonful at a time. In a small bowl, coarsely crush cube sugar. Dip top of each ball in sugar.

3. Place balls on lightly greased baking sheet. Bake in a preheated 350°F oven 10 to 15 minutes, or until golden brown. Cool on a wire rack.

NOTE: Store in an airtight container.

Old-fashioned Mincemeat Pie

A traditional Christmas treat, mincemeat pie came under Puritan attack in the seventeenth century as part of a "pagan" celebration. Fortunately the pie survived, and this recipe includes real meat, as in centuries past. *Yields 3 pies*

> 1½ *pounds lean beef, cut in 1-inch cubes*
> ½ *pound beef suet, finely chopped*
> 4 *cups golden raisins*
> 2 *cups currants*
> ¼ *cup chopped candied citron*
> ¼ *cup chopped orange peel*
> ¼ *cup chopped lemon peel*
> 4 *cups tart apples, peeled and coarsely chopped*
> 1 *cup granulated sugar*
> ½ *tablespoon ground cinnamon*
> ½ *tablespoon ground allspice*
> ½ *tablespoon ground nutmeg*
> ½ *tablespoon ground cloves*
> 2⅔ *cups brandy*
> 1½ *cups dry sherry*
> *(For pie crust ingredients, see page 4.)*
>
> *3 9-inch pie plates*

1. In a large pan, add enough water to cover the beef. Boil until tender enough to be shredded with a fork. In a large mixing bowl, combine beef, suet, raisins, currants, citron, fruit peels, apples, sugar, and spices. Stir thoroughly.

2. Pour brandy and sherry over the mixture. Mix. Cover the bowl and leave in a cool place, not the refrigerator, for 3 weeks. Each week, examine the mincemeat and moisten as necessary with brandy and sherry.

3. Make pie crust according to the instructions on page 4.

4. Fill pie crust with mincemeat. Roll out remaining dough ⅛ inch thick and ¼ inch wide. Place strips across top of pie, then

interweave other strips to form a lattice. Trim edges of lattice; seal; crimp.

5. Bake in a preheated 375°F oven 45 to 50 minutes, or until crust is golden brown.

NOTE: Extra mincemeat may be used in making Coventry god-cakes (see page 19).

Mince Pie (Meatless)

Mincemeat, however rich in other respects, is now commonly meatless. Such is the case with the filling for this pie. You will nevertheless find the pie a superb dessert, filled with the good things that make a mince pie such an important part of many Christmas dinners. *Yields 1 pie*

> 5 *tart apples, peeled and coarsely chopped*
> 1 *cup golden raisins*
> 1 *cup currants*
> 1½ *cups mixed candied fruit peel, diced*
> 1 *cup apple cider*
> 2 *cups dark brown sugar, firmly packed*
> ½ *teaspoon salt*
> 1 *teaspoon ground cinnamon*
> 1 *teaspoon ground nutmeg*
> 1 *teaspoon ground cloves*
> 1 *teaspoon ground allspice*
> ¼ *cup brandy*
> *(For pie crust ingredients, see page 4.)*
>
> *9-inch pie plate*

1. In a large saucepan, combine apples, raisins, currants, fruit peel, and apple cider. Bring to a boil and simmer, uncovered, about 20 minutes, until little liquid is left.

2. Add sugar, salt, and spices. Mix. Simmer about 10 minutes longer, or until thick. Add brandy.

3. Make pie crust according to the instructions on page 4.

4. Fill pie crust with mincemeat. Roll out remaining dough ⅛ inch thick and ¼ inch wide. Place strips across other strips to form a lattice. Trim edges of lattice; seal; crimp.

5. Bake in a preheated 375°F oven 40 to 50 minutes, or until crust is golden brown.

NOTE: The same mincemeat may be used in making Coventry god-cakes (see page 19).

Diples—Greek Christmas Folds

(thee-PLESS)

"Folds" here refers to the Christ Child's swaddling clothes. These fried pastries are a beloved Christmas treat in Greece. *Yields 4 dozen*

Honey Syrup
1½ cups honey
1 cup water
1 tablespoon ground cinnamon
½ teaspoon ground cloves
½ teaspoon grated orange rind
1 tablespoon orange extract

Pastry
3 eggs
⅔ cup lukewarm water
½ teaspoon salt
1 teaspoon aniseeds
2 tablespoons butter

3 cups all-purpose flour
vegetable oil for deep frying

Topping (optional—use any of the following)
⅓ cup sesame seeds, lightly toasted
¾ cup any finely chopped nuts
ground cinnamon
vanilla sugar (see page 5)

deep fryer or other deep pan for frying

1. To make syrup: In a saucepan, combine all syrup ingredients. Bring to a boil. Simmer 10 minutes. Cool before using.

2. In a large mixing bowl, combine eggs, water, salt, aniseeds, and butter. Mix thoroughly. Gradually add flour and mix. If sticky, add more flour.

3. On a lightly floured surface, knead dough until smooth. Roll out to ¼-inch thickness. With a pastry cutter, cut into 1½-inch squares. Fold squares in half diagonally to form triangles. Press the touching tips together lightly.

4. Heat oil to 375°F. Fry a few triangles at a time. Fry a minute or two until golden brown, turning once. Drain on paper towels. Transfer to a large platter.

5. Cover with cooled syrup. Cool before using. Sprinkle with your choice of topping.

Strufoli—Honey Balls

Deep-fried and coated with honey, strufoli are a classic Christmas dessert in Italy. A striking centerpiece for the Christmas table, they may be arranged as a pyramid, cone, or wreath. *Yields 10–12 servings*

2½ cups all-purpose flour
1 teaspoon baking powder
¼ teaspoon salt
1 teaspoon grated lemon rind
1 teaspoon grated orange rind
4 eggs
1 tablespoon vegetable oil
vegetable oil for deep frying

Honey Syrup
¾ cup honey
¼ cup water
¼ cup granulated sugar
1 tablespoon lemon juice

green and red candied cherries for garnish (optional)
multicolored sequins for garnish (optional)

deep fryer or other deep pan for frying

1. In a mixing bowl, combine flour, baking powder, salt, fruit rinds, eggs, and 1 tablespoon of vegetable oil. Mix thoroughly. If sticky, add more flour.

2. Knead dough until smooth. Roll out to ½-inch-thick rope. Cut into ¼-inch pieces.

3. Heat oil to 375°F. Fry a few balls at a time until golden brown. Drain on paper towels. Transfer to a large platter.

4. To make syrup: In a saucepan, combine honey, water, sugar, and lemon juice. Bring to a boil and simmer about 10 minutes.

5. Pour syrup over balls on platter. Garnish with cherries and/ or sequins if desired.

NOTE: May be stored in refrigerator up to a week.

Klenäter—Swedish Christmas Crullers

(kleh-NET-ter)

These crisp crullers from Sweden are also a Christmas tradition in several other countries—as Klejner in Denmark, Fattigmann in Norway, and Chrust in Poland. Note the delicate hints of lemon and brandy. *Yields about 5 dozen*

> 4 egg yolks
> ¼ cup confectioners' sugar
> ½ stick butter
> 2 cups all-purpose flour
> ¼ cup brandy
> 1 teaspoon grated lemon rind
> confectioners' sugar for sprinkling on top
>
> pastry wheel; deep fryer

1. In a mixing bowl, beat egg yolks and sugar until light and fluffy. Add remaining ingredients. Mix thoroughly. Cover dough and refrigerate overnight.

2. Roll out dough to ⅛-inch thickness. Using a pastry wheel, cut strips 1 inch wide and 3 inches long. Make a 1-inch slit down the middle. Fold one end through the slit and flatten.

3. Heat oil to 375°F. Place crullers in oil 4 or 5 at a time. When golden brown, turn over. Drain on paper towels. While still hot, sprinkle with confectioners' sugar. Sprinkle again with confectioners' sugar when about to serve.

NOTE: Store in an airtight container.

Shaker Christmas Pudding

This Shaker plum pudding, without candied fruit, is plainer than the more common version. But the pudding has a hearty, rich flavor all its own. *Yields 6–8 servings*

> 1 cup dark raisins
> ½ cup apple cider
> 3 cups all-purpose flour
> ½ teaspoon salt
> ½ teaspoon ground mace
> ½ tablespoon ground cinnamon
> ½ tablespoon ground ginger
> 1 cup beef suet, finely chopped
> 6 eggs, separated
> 1 cup milk
> ⅓ cup maple syrup

Soft Sauce
> 1 stick butter
> 1 cup light brown sugar, firmly packed
> 1 tablespoon rosewater

> 2-quart pudding mold

1. In a bowl, soak raisins in cider overnight. Drain and reserve cider. In a bowl, combine flour, salt, and spices. Toss and set aside.

2. In a mixing bowl, combine raisins, suet, egg yolks, milk, and maple syrup. Gradually add dry ingredients and reserved cider.

3. Beat egg whites until stiff peaks stand up. Fold into batter. Grease and flour mold. Pour pudding into mold. Snap cover tight. Place a rack in a large pot on top of stove. Put mold on rack.

4. Pour in boiling water ⅔ of the way up the sides of the mold. Cover. Boil, then lower heat. Simmer until a toothpick

comes out clean, about 3 hours. Add more boiling water as necessary.

5. Remove mold from pot. Cool pudding to room temperature. Wrap pudding in foil. Refrigerate at least 1 week.

6. To make sauce: In a mixing bowl, cream butter and sugar until light and fluffy. Add rosewater. Spoon promptly over pudding.

NOTE: To reheat pudding, place mold on rack in large pot. Pour in boiling water ⅔ of the way up the sides of the mold. Bring to a boil and simmer 2 hours. Remove mold from pot. Carefully remove pudding from mold onto serving plate.

Ambrosia

Ambrosia, "food of the gods," is an appropriate name for the delectable dessert given here. Traditionally many Southerners have finished Christmas dessert with this light concoction of pineapple, oranges, and coconut. *Yields 8–10 servings*

> 2 *cups shredded coconut, preferably fresh*
> 6 *oranges, peeled, sectioned, and seeded*
> 1 *medium-size ripe pineapple, cut into bite-size chunks*
> ¼–½ *cup confectioners' sugar (depending on degree of sweetness desired)*
>
> *large glass bowl*

In glass bowl, place a layer of ½ the coconut, a layer of orange sections, and a layer of pineapple chunks. Sprinkle with sugar. Add a top layer of the remaining coconut. Cover and chill about 4 hours.

Plum Pudding

You may not find it practical to haul in a Yule log or serve a boar's head on a platter, but you can bring Olde England to your Christmas with plum pudding. This Christmas classic has delighted the British for centuries, in humble cottages as well as in baronial halls. Enhance the pudding by flaming it or by serving hard sauce with it. *Yields 8–10 servings*

⅓ cup currants
⅓ cup golden raisins
¼ cup chopped mixed candied fruit peel
¼ cup chopped candied cherries
⅓ cup slivered blanched almonds
⅓ cup carrots, peeled and grated
⅓ cup apples, peeled, cored, and chopped
½ tablespoon grated orange peel
½ tablespoon grated lemon peel
1 cup beef suet, finely chopped
⅔ cup flour
¼ teaspoon ground cloves
¼ teaspoon ground nutmeg
¼ teaspoon ground cinnamon
½ teaspoon salt
1 cup fine white dry bread crumbs
½ cup dark brown sugar, firmly packed
1 egg
½ cup brandy
2 tablespoons orange juice
1 tablespoon lemon juice
1 cup brandy for flaming (optional)

2-quart pudding mold

1. In a mixing bowl, combine currants, raisins, mixed fruit peel, cherries, almonds, carrots, apples, orange and lemon peels, and beef suet. Mix thoroughly. (If necessary, use your hands.)

2. In another mixing bowl, combine flour, spices, salt, bread crumbs, and brown sugar. Mix. Add to fruit mixture.

3. In a third bowl, beat egg until light and fluffy. Add brandy and juices. Mix. Add this mixture to fruit mixture. Mix thoroughly. (Use hands and knead until thoroughly mixed.)

4. Cover dough with a damp cloth. Refrigerate at least 12 hours.

5. Grease mold and pour in pudding. Snap cover tight. Place a rack in a large pot on top of stove. Put mold on rack.

6. Pour in boiling water ⅔ of the way up the sides of the mold. Cover. Boil, then lower heat. Simmer until a toothpick comes out clean, about 4 hours. Add more boiling water as necessary.

7. Remove mold from pot. Cool pudding to room temperature. Wrap pudding in foil. Refrigerate at least 1 month.

Hard Sauce
1 stick butter
1⅓ cups confectioners' sugar
2–3 tablespoons brandy

In a bowl, cream butter and sugar until light and fluffy. Gradually beat in brandy. Place in serving dish and cover. Refrigerate.

To reheat pudding:
Place mold on rack in large pot. Pour in boiling water ⅔ of the way up the sides of the mold. Bring to a boil and simmer 2 hours. Remove mold from the pot. Carefully remove pudding from mold onto serving plate.

To serve pudding:
Stick a plastic sprig of holly in center of pudding. See page 253 for detailed flaming instructions.

Apple Yule Logs

Going far back into the English past, this dessert is unusual, tasty, and easy to make. Its appearance in a nest of blue flames adds a dramatic note to a Christmas celebration. *Yields 6 servings*

Filling
½ cup dark raisins, finely chopped
½ cup mixed candied fruit peel, finely chopped
2 tablespoons dark brown sugar, firmly packed
¼ cup finely ground bread crumbs
3 tablespoons whiskey

Syrup
1¼ cups granulated sugar
3 cups water
¼ teaspoon salt

6 large apples, peeled and cored
whiskey for flaming

baking dish large enough to hold 6 apples

1. To make filling: In a small bowl, combine raisins, mixed fruit peel, brown sugar, bread crumbs, and 3 tablespoons of whiskey. Mix thoroughly. Set aside.
2. To make syrup: In a saucepan, combine sugar, water, and salt. Boil 10 minutes. Allow to simmer 10 minutes more. Remove from heat and cool.
3. Peel and core apples 1¼ hours before serving. Place in greased baking dish. Stuff with filling. Pour syrup over apples. While baking, baste apples several times.
4. Bake in a preheated 275°F oven (so apples will not lose shape) 50 to 60 minutes, or until apples are tender. Pour or spoon off syrup into a small serving dish.
5. See page 253 for detailed flaming instructions. After a few moments, extinguish flames and serve. Top apples with syrup.

Irish Christmas Pudding

This Irish version of Christmas pudding is crammed with dried and candied fruits and laced with Irish whiskey. When flamed, it reaches the peak of moist, savory goodness. *Yields 1 pudding*

⅓ *cup currants*
⅓ *cup dark raisins*
⅓ *cup chopped citron*
⅓ *cup chopped candied cherries*
1½ *cups Irish whiskey*
⅔ *cup all-purpose flour*
2 *cups bread crumbs*
⅔ *cup light brown sugar, firmly packed*
1⅓ *cups finely chopped suet*
1 *teaspoon ground allspice*
1 *teaspoon ground nutmeg*
½ *teaspoon ground ginger*
⅔ *cup blanched almonds, coarsely chopped*
1 *apple, peeled and grated*
⅓ *cup lemon juice*
1 *teaspoon grated lemon rind*
4 *eggs*
1 *cup Guinness stout*
butter for greasing mold
extra Irish whiskey for soaking pudding and flaming

2-quart pudding mold; cheesecloth

1. In a bowl, combine currants, raisins, citron, cherries, and Irish whiskey. Cover and leave overnight.

2. In a mixing bowl, combine flour, bread crumbs, sugar, suet, and spices. Mix. Add almonds, apple, whiskey-soaked fruit, lemon juice, and lemon rind. Mix.

3. Beat eggs. Add Guinness. Mix. Gradually add to flour mixture. Mix thoroughly.

4. Grease mold. Pour pudding into mold. Snap cover tight on mold. Place on rack in a large kettle. Pour in water ⅔ of the way up the sides of the mold. Cover. Boil, then lower heat. Simmer until a toothpick comes out clean, about 4 hours. Add more boiling water as necessary.

5. Remove mold from kettle. Cool pudding to room temperature. Remove pudding from mold and place on plate. Pour Irish whiskey over pudding. After pudding soaks up whiskey, wrap in cheesecloth. Wrap in foil and refrigerate 2 or 3 weeks.

To reheat pudding:
Place mold on rack in large kettle. Pour in boiling water ⅔ of the way up the sides of the mold. Bring to a boil and simmer 2 hours. Remove mold from kettle. Carefully remove pudding from mold onto serving plate.

To serve pudding:
Warm 1 cup of Irish whiskey in pan without overheating. See page 253 for detailed instructions on flaming.

Ris à l'Amande—Danish Rice Pudding

(REES a la-MAHND)

This delightfully crunchy and nourishing rice-and-almond pudding is a favorite at Christmas celebrations in Denmark. Either plain or topped with Peter Heering or other cherry liqueur, this dessert is a sure hit. Include a whole almond if you wish—it's sure to bring good luck to the person who finds it in his or her portion. *Yields about 8–10 servings*

> 3½ cups milk
> ¾ cup long-grain white rice
> 3 tablespoons butter
> ⅓ cup confectioners' sugar
> ½ teaspoon salt
> ⅔ cup blanched almonds, coarsely chopped
> ¼ cup sweet sherry
> 1 teaspoon vanilla extract
> 1 whole blanched almond (optional)
> 1 cup heavy cream, whipped
> Peter Heering or cherry liqueur (optional)
>
> serving bowl

1. In a medium-size saucepan, heat milk until it boils. Stir in rice, butter, sugar, and salt. Cover; reduce heat and simmer rice about 25 minutes, until tender. (Don't allow to become mushy.) Cool.

2. Stir in almonds, sherry, vanilla, and, if desired, whole almond. Fold cream into rice mixture.

3. Pour into serving bowl. Chill. When serving, top with liqueur if desired.

Jul Gulerod Kage Budding—
Christmas Carrot Cake Pudding

(YUL GUH-le-rowth KAY-ya BOO-thing)

With a consistency like that of a plum pudding, this "cake-pudding" is a cherished Scandinavian favorite. Grated raw carrot is combined with spices, dried fruits, and chopped nuts to make a dessert that will delight your Christmas guests. *Yields 1 cake.*

1 *stick butter*
1 *cup dark brown sugar, firmly packed*
2 *eggs*
1¾ *cups grated carrots*
½ *cup golden raisins*
¼ *cup candied lemon peel, finely chopped*
¼ *cup candied orange peel, finely chopped*
1⅔ *cups all-purpose flour*
½ *teaspoon baking soda*
½ *tablespoon baking powder*
½ *teaspoon salt*
1 *teaspoon ground cinnamon*
½ *teaspoon ground nutmeg*
½ *teaspoon ground allspice*
½ *teaspoon ground cardamom*
sweetened whipped cream for topping

6-cup Bundt pan

1. In a mixing bowl, cream butter and sugar until light and fluffy. Add eggs and mix. Add remaining ingredients except whipped cream. Mix thoroughly.

2. Place in greased Bundt pan. Bake in a preheated 350°F oven about 1 hour, or until a cake tester comes out clean. Cool on a wire rack.

NOTE: Serve with whipped cream on top.

French Chocolate Truffles

Enjoyed throughout the year in France, chocolate truffles become especially popular at Christmastime. Try them with coffee after your Christmas dinner. *Yields 3½ dozen*

> 1 *cup heavy cream*
> 12 *squares semisweet chocolate, cut into pieces*
> 2 *tablespoons Grand Marnier*
> *unsweetened cocoa powder for coating*
>
> *shallow pan*

1. In a saucepan, boil cream. Remove from heat. Add chocolate and stir until completely melted. Stir in Grand Marnier.
2. Put in a shallow pan and refrigerate 3 to 4 hours, until chocolate hardens.
3. Sprinkle cocoa on a sheet of wax paper. Shape into balls slightly less than 1 inch in diameter. Roll balls in cocoa. Refrigerate.

NOTES: May be prepared several weeks in advance and frozen.
May be served in tiny fluted candy cups.

Marzipan Christmas Figurines

For centuries, marzipan has brightened Christmas in Germany and Denmark. Shaped into animals, vegetables, flowers, and other natural forms, marzipan figurines have charmed generations of children. Marzipan pigs especially are associated with Christmas. *Yields about 3 dozen*

> *8 ounces almond paste, storebought or homemade (see page 4)*
> *2 egg whites, unbeaten*
> *3¼ cups confectioners' sugar*
> *½ teaspoon almond extract*
> *food coloring*

In a mixing bowl, mix almond paste and egg whites until well blended. Gradually add sugar and almond extract. Mix until smooth. Add more sugar if marzipan is too sticky. Add a few drops of water if marzipan is too dry. Cover with plastic wrap and refrigerate a day or two before using.

To shape figurines:
When modeling marzipan, dust hands and working surface lightly with confectioners' sugar.

Pig: Add food coloring to make marzipan pink. Make pig 2 inches long. Use chocolate or bits of candy for the eyes.

Fruits and Vegetables: To make uniform sizes of fruits, form marzipan rope about 1 inch in diameter. Cut into 1-inch lengths. Roll pieces between hands to form balls. Shape into fruits and vegetables, starting with those that are lighter colored.

For lemon, tint marzipan yellow. Shape into oval pointed at ends. Roll on grater to simulate roughened skin.

For banana, tint marzipan yellow. Roll into curved, tapered shape. Dissolve a little cocoa in water and paint on streaks.

For pear, tint marzipan green. Make pear shape. Add reddish blush on one side.

For lime, do as with lemon only in green.

For apple, color marzipan red or yellow. Use whole clove for stem.

For orange, tint marzipan orange. Use grater to texture skin. Push whole clove into stem end.

For potato, shape uncolored marzipan. Roll in dark cocoa. Press in eyes with toothpick.

Use your imagination for other fruits and vegetables.

NOTE: After shaping, dry on a wire rack. Store in an airtight container.

Sokolates—Greek Chocolate Bells

(so-ko-LAH-tes)

These candies grace Greek tables at Christmastime. They're a superb blend of chocolate, nuts, cream, and rum. *Yields about 6 dozen*

> 1 *pound sweet chocolate*
> 2 *cups ground pecans*
> 3¼ *cups confectioners' sugar*
> 3 *tablespoons light cream*
> 1½ *tablespoons rum flavoring or 3 tablespoons rum confectioners' sugar for coating*
>
> *serving plate*

1. Place pieces of chocolate in a double boiler and melt. Mix in pecans, sugar, cream, and rum. Mix thoroughly.

2. When cool, shape balls of dough about 1 inch across into little bells. Roll in sugar. Chill.

Turron de Yema—Mexican Egg Yolk Nougat

(too-ROHN day YAY-ma)

These rich candies are a treat popular in Mexico after Christmas dinner. The chopped nuts on top are optional, added as much for appearance as for flavor. *Yields 77*

> 2½ *cups blanched almonds, finely ground*
> 2¾ *cups confectioners' sugar*
> 6 *egg yolks*
> 1 *tablespoon ground cinnamon*
> 1 *tablespoon grated lemon rind*
> *coarsely chopped almonds for top (optional)*
>
> 7 × 11-*inch pan*

Mix ingredients. Line pan with wax paper. Fill with mixture. Pat smooth. Cover with wax paper. Place something flat on top, weight, and refrigerate several hours. Add chopped almonds if desired. Cut into 1-inch squares.

NOTE: Will keep for several weeks.

Meringue Mushrooms

Eaten by themselves as candy or served along with Bûche de Noël (see page 164), these charming mushrooms are always a delight at the Christmas table. *Yields 4½ dozen, depending on size*

Mushrooms
2 egg whites
⅛ teaspoon salt
⅓ cup granulated sugar
½ teaspoon almond extract
cocoa for sprinkling on top

Frosting
1 cup confectioners' sugar
1 tablespoon butter
hot water
½ teaspoon almond extract

baking sheet; pastry bag; ¼-inch round tube

1. In a mixing bowl, mix egg whites until they form soft peaks. Add salt, sugar, and almond extract. Continue beating until stiff peaks stand up.

2. Lightly grease and flour baking sheet. Put tube in pastry bag. Fill bag with meringue. With tube held upright, pipe out mushroom caps 1 to 1½ inches in diameter, using about half of meringue. Sprinkle cocoa over top of mushroom caps.

3. Pipe out stems in varying sizes ½ to 1 inch long. Taper stems at one end. Bake caps and stems in a preheated 200°F oven 1½ hours. Remove from oven and cool on a wire rack.

4. To make frosting: Combine ingredients. Mix thoroughly. Set aside.

5. Assemble mushrooms: With a paring knife, gently make depressions in bottom of caps. Dip pointed ends of stems in frosting. Insert ends into depressions under caps. Serve in candy dish or use to decorate Bûche de Noël.

Meringue Kisses

Watch these easy-to-make cookies disappear almost as fast as they were made! Chocolate chips and nuts in a wispy meringue are an irresistible addition to the Christmas cookie platter. *Yields 2 dozen*

> 2 *egg whites*
> 1/8 *teaspoon salt*
> 2/3 *cup confectioners' sugar*
> 2/3 *cup semisweet chocolate morsels, bits, or chips*
> 1/3 *cup coarsely chopped pecans*
>
> *baking sheet*

1. Preheat oven to 350°F. In a mixing bowl, beat egg whites until foamy. Add salt and gradually add sugar 1 tablespoon at a time, beating until very stiff. Fold in chocolate morsels and nuts.

2. Spread parchment paper on baking sheet. (Or lightly grease baking sheet.) Drop by teaspoonfuls on prepared sheet. Place close together—they won't spread. Put in oven and *turn off heat*. Leave overnight.

NOTE: Best when served fresh; they don't keep well.

27

OTHER FESTIVE DESSERTS

The holidays covered in this book represent only a fraction of feast days and other times of special rejoicing throughout the year. National holidays (frequently of independence), local holidays commemorating events of regional importance, additional religious holidays, and even personal holidays are other occasions that can be fun to celebrate with a special menu, including a suitably festive dessert.

The recipes in this chapter are either associated with several holidays or are simply festive in themselves. Try them for classic desserts you will enjoy again and again—such as biscuit tortoni, baklavá, cannoli, and croquembouche—holiday or no holiday!

Croquembouche

(croke-em-BOOSH)

This highly ornamental dessert consists of cream puffs that have been glazed (hence the name, which means "crunch in the mouth"). Heaped in pyramid fashion, croquembouche makes a stunning centerpiece for the holiday table. *Yields 1 pyramid*

Puffs
1½ cups water
1½ sticks butter
1⅔ cups all-purpose flour
1 teaspoon salt
6 eggs

1 egg beaten with 1 tablespoon water for glaze

Pastry Cream
4 egg yolks
1½ cups granulated sugar
¼ cup all-purpose flour
¼ teaspoon salt
1 cup light cream
1 teaspoon vanilla extract
2 tablespoons cognac

Caramel Syrup
2 cups granulated sugar
¾ cup water
¼ teaspoon cream of tartar

baking sheet; pastry bag with ½-inch round tube and ¼-inch round tube; pastry brush

1. In a saucepan, bring water and butter to a boil. Lower heat. Add flour and salt, stirring constantly until mixture leaves sides of

pan and forms a ball. Remove from heat. Add eggs 1 at a time, beating after each addition.

2. Grease baking sheet. Put ½-inch round tube in pastry bag. Squeeze out mounds of pastry 1½ inches in diameter and 1 inch high, spaced 2 inches apart. Using pastry brush, glaze each puff with egg glaze. Smooth top of each puff.

3. Bake in a preheated 400°F oven 20 minutes. After removing from oven, pierce puffs with a sharp knife. Return puffs to oven 10 minutes. Cool on a wire rack.

4. To make pastry cream: In a saucepan, beat egg yolks. Gradually add sugar. Beat in flour, salt, and cream over medium heat. Stir until mixture thickens. Remove from heat.

5. Add vanilla and cognac. Cool completely. Using ¼-inch tube, pipe pastry cream into puffs.

6. To make caramel syrup: In a saucepan, combine sugar, water, and cream of tartar. Over medium heat bring mixture to a boil and continue boiling until syrup is a light caramel color. Remove from heat.

7. Dip each puff into syrup and arrange on a plate to form a pyramid or cone. Serve same day.

NOTE: Cream puffs and pastry cream can be made the day before. But do not fill puffs until the day of serving.

Cannoli

A filled pastry, cannoli are a festive treat from Italy that just about everyone loves. Fillings vary, but I recommend the rich ricotta-cheese concoction given here. *Yields 18*

Filling
3 cups ricotta cheese
1½ cups confectioners' sugar
½ teaspoon grated lemon rind
¼ cup semisweet chocolate morsels, bits, or chips
1 teaspoon vanilla extract
½ cup candied citron or candied orange peel, finely chopped

Shells
2 cups all-purpose flour
1 tablespoon granulated sugar
¼ teaspoon salt
1 tablespoon vegetable shortening
2 tablespoons white vinegar
2 tablespoons cold water
2 eggs
1 egg white for brushing
⅓ cup pistachio nuts for ends (optional)
confectioners' sugar for coating

cannoli forms; deep fryer or other deep pan for frying; pastry bag with large plain tip

1. To make filling: Beat ricotta cheese until smooth. Add remaining ingredients. Mix and chill.

2. To make shells: In a mixing bowl, combine flour, sugar, and salt. With a pastry blender, cut in shortening until pieces of dough are small.

3. Add vinegar, water, and eggs. Mix well. On a lightly

floured surface, knead dough until smooth, 5 to 10 minutes. Shape into a ball. Cover dough with plastic wrap. Chill in refrigerator 1 hour.

4. On a lightly floured surface, roll out dough to ⅛-inch thickness. Cut into 4½-inch circles. Using a rolling pin, roll circles into ovals. Roll dough loosely around cannoli forms. Brush edges with egg white; seal. Slightly flare ends of dough.

5. Heat oil to 350°F. Fry 2 or 3 at a time for a minute or two, or until golden brown. Drain on paper towels *5 seconds only.* Carefully remove cannoli forms. Cool shells completely.

6. With pastry bag or a spoon, fill shells. If desired, sprinkle pistachio nuts on ends. Dust with confectioners' sugar.

NOTE: Store unfilled shells in an airtight container. Fill shells when ready to serve.

Cherries Jubilee

For a spectacular finale to a holiday dinner, it would be hard to beat this dessert of flaming cherries over ice cream. *Yields 6 servings*

> ⅓ *cup red currant jelly*
> 16-*ounce can pitted black cherries, drained (reserve juice)*
> 4 *tablespoons cherry juice*
> ¾ *cup cognac*
> 1 *quart vanilla ice cream*
>
> *chafing dish*

In chafing dish, melt jelly. Add cherries and juice. In a saucepan, heat cognac for flaming (see page 253). Pour flaming cognac over cherries and juice. Serve over ice cream in individual dishes.

Linzertorte

This cake, which originated in Linz, northern Austria, is a rich confection of raspberry jam in an almond-flavored crust. *Yields 1 cake*

> 1½ *sticks butter*
> ½ *cup confectioners' sugar*
> 2 *eggs*
> ½ *teaspoon salt*
> ½ *tablespoon grated lemon rind*
> ½ *teaspoon ground cinnamon*
> ¼ *teaspoon ground cloves*
> 1⅓ *cups unblanched almonds, finely ground*
> 1⅓ *cups all-purpose flour*
> *raspberry jam*
> 1 *egg yolk, beaten, for glaze*
> *confectioners' sugar for sprinkling on top*
>
> 9 × *1-inch false-bottom cake pan*

1. In a large mixing bowl, cream butter and sugar until light and fluffy. Add eggs 1 at a time, beating after each addition. Add salt, lemon rind, cinnamon, cloves, almonds, and flour. Mix thoroughly. Chill overnight.

2. Set aside ⅓ of the dough. Press remaining dough into cake pan with the dough to the top of the sides.

3. Spread jam evenly on top of the dough. Take the reserved dough and roll out to ⅛-inch thickness. Cut ½-inch-wide strips. Form into lattice over jam. Brush the lattice with egg yolk glaze. Bake in a preheated 350°F oven 40 to 50 minutes, or until lightly browned. Sprinkle with confectioners' sugar.

Baklavá

One of the great Middle Eastern contributions to world cuisine, baklavá is a heavenly blend of flaky dough, ground nuts, and honey. Traditional in Greece and other countries for New Year's as well as other festive occasions, baklavá makes *any* meal festive. *Yields about 2½ dozen 2 × 2-inch pieces*

Syrup
1⅓ cups granulated sugar
1⅓ cups water
1 cup honey
1 tablespoon orange-flower water (optional)*

Filling
3 cups walnuts, pecans, or almonds (or mixture of
*   these), finely ground*
1 teaspoon ground cinnamon
½ teaspoon ground cloves
½ teaspoon ground nutmeg

3 sticks butter, melted
1 pound phyllo dough (for handling, read directions
*   on the box)*

13 × 9 × 2-inch baking dish

1. To make syrup: In a saucepan, boil sugar and water 5 minutes. Remove from heat. Stir in honey. Cool. Add orange-flower water. Set aside.

2. In a mixing bowl, combine nuts and spices. Toss and set aside.

3. Grease baking dish. Unfold phyllo dough sheets. To pre-

---

* Available in some gourmet shops, pharmacies, and suppliers of Middle Eastern foods.

vent drying, cover with a damp towel. Place a phyllo dough sheet over pan. Brush with melted butter. Repeat 6 times.

4. Sprinkle ½ of nut mixture evenly over top. Add 7 more layers of phyllo dough, brushing with butter in between. Top with remaining nut filling. Place remaining phyllo sheets on top, brushing with butter in between.

5. With a sharp-pointed knife, cut top layers of phyllo dough into diamond-shaped pieces. Bake in a preheated 350°F oven. Bake 1 to 1½ hours, or until golden brown.

6. With a sharp-pointed knife, cut through *entire* pastry along previous diagonal lines. Pour syrup over pastry. Cool.

Schwarzwälder Kirschtorte— Black Forest Cherry Cake

Some have called this superb cake, originally from the Black Forest region, Germany's most famous dessert. Certainly few desserts anywhere surpass its cherry-drenched chocolaty lusciousness. *Yields 1 cake*

Chocolate Curls
8-ounce bar semisweet chocolate

Cake
1¾ cups all-purpose flour
1 teaspoon baking powder
½ teaspoon salt
2 ounces semisweet chocolate
1 stick butter
¾ cup granulated sugar
4 eggs
1 teaspoon almond extract

Filling and Topping

2 *cups whipping cream*
⅔ *cup confectioners' sugar*
⅓ *cup kirsch*
16-*ounce can pitted red tart cherries, drained (reserve
   liquid)*
12 *maraschino cherries with stems*

2 *9-inch round cake pans; pastry bag with star tube*

1. To make chocolate curls: Chocolate should be at room temperature (but not soft) to ensure best slicing. With a vegetable peeler, shave curls off bar. Refrigerate until ready to use.

2. To make cake: In a bowl, combine flour, baking powder, and salt. Toss and set aside. In a double boiler, melt chocolate over low heat. Cool.

3. In a mixing bowl, cream butter and sugar until light and fluffy. Add eggs 1 at a time, beating after each addition.

4. Add melted chocolate and gradually the flour mixture. Add almond extract. Pour batter into greased and floured cake pans. Bake in a preheated 350°F oven 30 to 35 minutes, or until a cake tester comes out clean. Cool in pan 5 minutes, then on a wire rack. Cut each layer horizontally, to make four layers.

5. To make filling and topping: In a mixing bowl, beat cream until stiff. Gradually add confectioners' sugar. Sprinkle ⅓ of kirsch on a layer of the cake. Cover with whipped cream and add ⅓ of drained cherries. Place a second layer on top and repeat. Then a third.

6. Top the cake with the fourth layer. Spread ⅔ of remaining whipped cream on the top and sides of the cake. Place last of whipped cream in pastry bag. Pipe rosettes of whipped cream around the top edge of the cake. Top rosettes with cherries. Garnish top center and sides with chocolate curls.

Biscuit Tortoni

Named for one Tortoni, a restaurateur in nineteenth-century Paris, this frozen dessert has long been a favorite on festive occasions. *Yields 12 servings*

> 1½ *cups heavy cream*
> ½ *cup confectioners' sugar*
> 1 *cup crumbs of macaroons or vanilla wafers*
> 2 *tablespoons sherry or dark rum*
> ¼ *cup chopped toasted almonds*
> 1 *teaspoon vanilla extract*
> 6 *candied cherries, cut in half*
>
> *medium-size muffin tin; paper cupcake liners*

    1. Place cupcake liners in muffin tin. In a mixing bowl, beat cream and sugar until stiff. Set aside 3 tablespoons of macaroon or vanilla wafer crumbs. Add remaining crumbs to sugar-and-cream mixture. Fold in sherry, almonds, and vanilla.

    2. Spoon cream mixture into paper liners. (You can use an ice cream scoop.) Sprinkle tops with reserved crumbs. Top each with a candied cherry half. Freeze until firm, at least 4 hours.

28

PRESENTING DESSERTS ATTRACTIVELY

The ideal holiday dessert is as appealing to the eyes, and even minds, of diners as to their palates. Of course, the holiday spirit itself sets the mood for enjoying an appropriate dessert. But you can enhance the effect of your desserts by planning how to present them. Here are some ideas you may find useful.

Place Settings

The place setting for your dessert can give it eye appeal that displays its festiveness. For example, a neutral-colored dessert looks more attractive on a vividly colored plate. Desserts with bright colors harmonize better with plates in quieter hues. Typically a holiday is the time when you bring out your fine china, which is sure to enhance the serving of a dessert. Yet consider decorated paper plates, mats, and napkins for more informal holidays such as Halloween.

In addition, you can add a holiday touch to your place setting with candies suited to the holiday, such as Pennsylvania Dutch coconut eggs for Easter or marzipan pigs for Christmas (see pages 101 and 236, respectively). Other such candies can be readily bought.

Holiday Decorations

Look through a party shop or department store at the appropriate season to find ideas for holiday decorations. Some commercial decorations for different holidays are figurines (Pilgrim, pumpkin, Santa Claus, sleigh, Easter egg, rabbit, cupid, etc.), napkins and tablecloths and plates with holiday motifs, party favors, streamers, and wall decorations. Or try natural decorations such as pumpkins, gourds, holly, pine cones, evergreen sprays, flowers, and autumn leaves. Further decorations might include a menorah (Hanukkah candlestick), a crèche, colored eggs, flags, or a cardboard skeleton.

Centerpieces and Displays

Some desserts are natural centerpieces. What could be more charming on a Christmas table than a gingerbread house (see page 171)? Bûche de Noël (Christmas log) with meringue mushrooms (see pages 164 and 239 respectively) will add another delicious Christmasy note. Teiglach (see page 112); honey-covered fried or baked dough balls (for Rosh Hashanah), are often heaped in a cone or pyramid from which guests help themselves. Schwarzwälder Kirschtorte (Black Forest Cherry Cake) is still another striking centerpiece (see page 248).

Candied fruit, nuts, and candies such as gumdrops may be used on the holiday table to add festive touches. Try a bow on top of a tray handle to keynote the serving of a dessert. Or wrap a cake in ribbon to make it look like a Christmas package.

Containers can be chosen to enhance the presentation of a dessert and make it the focus of a holiday table. Cookies and candies can be served in glass jars either of ordinary design or in shapes such as a Christmas tree. Fancy baskets of many types add eye appeal to desserts. Try trays, single or of more than one tier, to display desserts of many kinds.

Scores of desserts in this book look attractive enough by themselves to grace any sideboard or dinner table. Use your imagination to brighten the presentation of holiday desserts even further.

Flaming Desserts

Flaming a dessert can be an exercise in frustration or it can be the prelude to a joyous holiday scene with the faces of expectant guests illuminated only by the deep blue flame on a plum pudding or the traditional English flamed Apple Yule Log (see pages 228 and 230, respectively). Experience helps in flaming, but the directions here, based on those of the Cognac Bureau of Information, will ensure success.

1. Warm cognac (or other whiskey, if used) in a small metal pan over low heat.

2. Remove cognac from heat when it is warm to the touch. Do *not* overheat; this could cause the cognac to ignite spontaneously.

3. Light with a wooden match, not a book match.

4. Stand back. Ignite the vapors (touching match to liquid will douse the flame).

5. Pour flaming cognac gently over dessert.

6. Do *not* pour additional cognac on the cognac flame in pan or on dessert. Flame could travel up to the bottle.

Additional tip: To promote flaming, sprinkle a little sugar on dessert before pouring cognac.

Background Information

Many of the desserts in this book, and all the holidays, have interesting stories behind them. Give your guests the background cited in the chapter introductions! Twelfth Night, often ignored today, is rich in such traditional lore. The finding of a bean or other token in Twelfth Night cakes (making the finder a leader of the revels) offers an opportunity for diversion based on centuries of tradition. Consult an encyclopedia or visit a library for more holiday details that will entertain your guests.

The preceding ideas cover only some of the elements that go into the attractive presentation of desserts. With a little ingenuity, you can come up with additional gracious touches of your own.

INDEX